W9-DIA-538

FORGING THE AMERICAN CHARACTER

FORGING THE AMERICAN CHARACTER

Edited by JAMES W. HALL
State University of New York at Albany

HOLT, RINEHART AND WINSTON
New York • Chicago • San Francisco • Atlanta
Dallas • Montreal • Toronto • London • Sydney

Cover illustration: Immigrants aboard ship, 1902. Photo by William H. Rau. *(Library of Congress)*

Library of Congress Catalog Card Number: 77-131928
SBN: 03-077540-X
Printed in the United States of America
1 2 3 4 45 9 8 7 6 5 4 3 2 1

CONTENTS

Vermont Lawyer, oil painting by Horace Bundy, 1841. *(Collection Edgar William and Bernice Chrysler Garbisch; National Gallery of Art, Washington, D.C.)*

INTRODUCTION

America begins in Europe. The American today is the descendant of immigrants, most of whom embarked upon their pioneering venture from Great Britain and the continent of Europe. American culture and character are inextricably linked by an historical bond to a common European background and heritage. But if American culture began in Europe, it is equally true that it does not end there. The American is not a European. His behavioral patterns are unmistakably different. Indeed by the nineteenth century, Americans had developed sufficiently distinctive characteristics from the peoples of western Europe to attract the attention of travelers and journalists and to invite examination and analysis by serious observers and writers, both foreign and native. Whether a European commentator such as Alexis de Tocqueville or a native American historian such as George Bancroft, these observers generally agreed that the American character was a unique and fascinating variation of the older European culture.

From the first settlements the American aboriginals were wholly excluded from participation in the developing society, and the dominant, most influential people were Englishmen who established themselves during the seventeenth and eighteenth centuries along the narrow strip of land east of the Appalachians. Predominantly English at the outset, the nature of the American character was also shaped by a physical environment that demanded new solutions to the problems of everyday living. At the same time the repeated influx of large numbers of additional settlers of varied cultural background brought instability, compromise, and change. The result of all this ferment was the emergence of a people neither European nor totally non-European, but American. Essentially a variation of the Western model, the American was nonetheless clearly distinguishable from his counterpart in France, Germany, England, or Greece.

Precisely what influences were responsible for the creation of this distinctive character during the formative years of the Republic? Which influences operative during the periods of historical settlement and growth as a nation were most significant in distinguishing the American way of thinking, doing, and conceptualizing from the ways of other peoples? An understanding of how such forces acted and interacted, and the degree to which each was significant in the process of cultural adaptation and systematization, is an important aspect in the study of the American people. The impact of these elements is largely responsible for the peculiarity and uniqueness of American history.

The introductory essay of this collection by Thomas L. Hartshorne provides a better understanding of national character and suggests both the limitations of the concept and ways in which it may be appropriately applied. Hartshorne cautions that descriptions of national character are useful generalizations and descriptions of tendencies only. Nevertheless he points out that the culture does influence individual differences in subtle ways, making possible large areas of group near-uniformity. His description of the concerns and problems of past studies provides a useful introduction to the other essays in this collection and calls attention to the study of national character as one of the important areas of investigation for scholars today.

The remaining essays of this collection are arranged in three general groups. The first focuses on the influence of the European cultural heritage upon the American character; the second stresses the importance of the American physical and social environment; the third group measures the effect of special opportunities offered by the New World.

One of the most pervasive and observable forces which shape a people is the cultural heritage—a body of learned systematic concepts, actions, and customs, shared by the group, and passed from parent to child. In a stable environment this heritage changes very little. The authors in the first group of articles agree that although the capacity of the American people to endure was indeed tested by their departure from the homes where they had been reared, and by their migration over vast expanses of water and wilderness to face a strange and sometimes hostile land, the cultural baggage which they carried with them remained the strength that enabled them to confront their strange environment and create a new life modeled on the culture they had known in the old country or "back east."

In the second selection the French observer Alexis de Tocqueville demonstrates that there was not an American opinion, custom, or law which could not be traced to the origins of a people. For most Americans, such origins were found in the institutions, practices, and language of England. The two greatest contributions from the English cultural heritage were a "spirit of religion" and a "spirit of liberty." He concludes that the English character of the earliest settlers, especially those of New England, spread to the whole American world, interpenetrating the culture and character of all those who came afterward. Does Tocqueville believe, however, that the American character was simply a transplantation of the English character, or was the American character unique by virtue of its *selection* of English elements? If selectivity is the essence of uniqueness, what other factors have determined the selection process? Does his distinction between the character of New Englanders and Southerners contradict his general thesis?

The third essay, by Edward Eggleston, is one of the earliest investigations of the manner in which English institutions were transported to America. First published in 1900, the study seeks to discover the origins of Anglo-Saxon culture in America. This culture, Eggleston argues, arrived as "mental furniture" with the early English emigrants; and it is to these first settlers that the dominant English traditions can be traced. If, however, American cultural traditions are indeed strongly influenced by their English background, does Eggleston offer any satisfactory explanation for the essential differences which exist today between the Englishman and the American?

The English background is further explored by Thomas Cuming Hall, who sees the origins of the American character is the "mists and half-lights of the days of King Edward III in England." This English heritage is not simply Puritanism, as Tocqueville maintains, nor may it be properly defined as Anglo-Saxonism, as Eggleston describes it, but rather it is the very old dissenting tradition of England. Hall sees as a contributing factor to American behavior the old English radical Protestantism, in which the individual could interpret the Scriptures and find salvation without need of church or clergy. Since his study is, however, primarily limited to the religious thought of Americans, one must ask whether his assumptions are applicable to other aspects of American life. Is American character largely indebted to just a single tradition in the English heritage?

In "Civilization in Transit," Dixon Ryan Fox develops Eggleston's approach further and sees the movement of culture as a continuing process that was far more important in the building of a great civilization than simply the efforts of self-reliant frontiersmen. His is a study of the transplantation of "professional competence" to America. But does Fox fully grasp the significance of Eggleston's thesis? Is it just certain institutions, professional skills, achievements in the arts and education that constitute the cultural heritage? Or were ideas and certain learned conceptual processes more germane to the formation of American character?

Louis B. Wright attempts to explore these basic conceptual processes. The "sturdiest and most lasting qualities" of Americans, including our pragmatically-oriented mode of thinking, our ideas of nationality and individualism, and our piety and morality, are all dominant character traits transmitted by the English cultural heritage. In Wright's analysis, this English influence is so pervasive that "it subtly determines qualities of mind and character in Americans who cannot claim a drop of Anglo-Saxon blood." Are such assertions defensible, however, in view of environmental forces which reshaped so many English ways of doing things? Did the English background contribute the most basic attitudes and traits of the American character or was it conditioned more by environmentally caused variations and alterations?

Oscar Handlin's well-known study *The Uprooted* presents the saga of the immigrants who came to America. The selection reprinted in this collection presents a poetic evocation of the mental and psychological state of the immigrant mind. Handlin relates the world view of the peasant to the situation he confronted in the New World and finds that the entire process led to conservatism, to a ready acceptance of tradition and authority.

Irrespective of national origin or class, education or occupation prior to immigration to America, all the new settlers and their descendants had to come to terms with the American physical and social environment. Faced with extremes of climate unknown in Europe, a vast and sparsely populated expanse of land, and a natural state unfettered by restrictive social institutions that characterized the Old World, these transplanted Europeans were required by necessity to find new solutions to the daily problems of life. Many writers believe the American environment, with its frontier conditions and abundance of bountiful land, has been the most significant force in forging American culture and character. The second group of essays is concerned with this "frontier thesis."

Essentially the frontier thesis argues that American character is best explained by rapid westward expansion which repeatedly brought American settlers into confrontation with an ever-retreating frontier. Frederick Jackson Turner, the most famous scholar to present this argument, saw American history as a process of constant social and institutional modification. The American environment exerted its influence upon both the newly arrived European and on Americans moving westward across the continent. The process occurred in definable sociological phases which were repeated over and over again as the line of settlement moved west. To Turner the great undercurrents of society were more important than political or personal history. He suggested that the frontier was a key to American history and one could understand American character only by a study of "the reactions between American society and the American environment." Many of the later scholars developing the frontier thesis were less cautious than Turner and accepted his hypothesis as an historical postulate. To them the frontier was not merely one force but the *only* force responsible for American character. For more than twenty years during the early twentieth century the Turner thesis went virtually unchallenged, and the scholarship produced on this topic by those who sought either to substantiate or later to discredit the theory comprises one of the richest and most important bodies of American historical literature. How inclusive is Turner's hypothesis? Does he define his frontier carefully and show specifically how it influenced the formation of national character? Were the forests and plains of America really more significant than the heritage brought from England and Europe?

Fifty-nine years after Turner presented his frontier hypothesis, Walter Prescott Webb expanded the application of the idea into a more universally applicable cultural theorem. Webb accepts the basic concept that the frontier profoundly affected Americans. He carries the hypothesis further by examining it in comparison to other historical frontier situations. The frontier experience, he says, whether found in the American West, African jungle, or Australian bush, is repeated over and over again as "the little Easts" gradually move into and consume "the greater Wests." What does Webb mean by interaction between the "Metropolis" and the "great Frontier"? Does his all-inclusive argument tend to support or weaken the assertion that American character is unique? Using Webb's formulation, can one defend environmental determination of national character?

In the next two essays Carl N. Degler and Ray Allen Billington review the scholarship that has followed in the wake of Turner's thesis. While Billington finds new support for the theory, Degler finds its importance exaggerated. He agrees that a new environment is selective: "Some of the European ways would wither; some would strike new root; still others would change and adapt to the new environment." But, Degler argues, after the first century of settlement the mold was set, and the pattern of Americans for generations to come was established. The frontier did provide an opportunity for new ideas to be tried, but it was not their place of origin. Whether the frontier was a place of opportunity or not, the fact that nineteenth-century Americans believed it to be so had an important influence upon the attitudes and character of Americans. But, is this writer justified in comparing the American frontier experience with that of the twelfth-century Germans, the South African Boers, or the Russians? What other factors might account for diverse practices among English and German settlers of the American land? And can the belief of a people in frontier opportunity be sustained when confrontation with reality may discredit such a belief?

Ray Allen Billington, upholding Turner's argument, sees in the frontier a social environment which weakened traditional control and values and made for experimentation and change in the way of life. If the frontier did not affect major alterations in the personalities or behavior patterns of frontiersmen, it nevertheless affected numerous modifications which became important and distinguishing qualities of American character. These factors were most noticeable in the West. For Billington it is competition, stimulated by the American social environment, which conditions the American character. Although Billington carefully reexamines other theories pertaining to the molding of American character, he sees all of these as stemming immediately or remotely from the Turner thesis. Ultimately, he says, the irreducible fact was the presence of unoccupied land that created a frontier social environment, which is the most important influence upon American character. This selection is also helpful in defining such concepts as national character, group personality, and interpersonal and cultural relationships.

Basic to any evaluation of the second group of essays is the determination whether accommodation to the American environment required only modest adaptations in the patterns of daily existence, or whether it required essential and far-reaching personality changes that made the American fundamentally different, or, as Hector St. John de Crèvecoeur, the French-American farmer, phrased it, a "new man."

If the first and second sets of essays deal primarily with those forces that for the American were inescapable—the cultural past he could not repudiate and the new environment he could not avoid—the essays in the last section describe a variety of character-molding forces or conditions arising from the fortunate confluence of heritage and environment. Although these elements defy neat categorization, one may say that they represent conditions of mind arising from life in a nation which seemed to offer unbounded opportunity.

One such element is *abundance,* and David Potter maintains that this is the most significant factor affecting Americans. Potter is one of a number of scholars who, through attention to quantifiable behavioral factors, has sought to enhance the historical perspective on the problem of character variations. For Potter the ideas of both Turner and Webb, while not inaccurate when applied to a certain stage of national development, are limited by myopic attention to the frontier experience. "Abundance in any form, including the frontier form, rather than the frontier in any unique sense," is the force "which wrought some of the major results in the American experience." But does Potter's emphasis on expanding technological abundance apply to the formative eighteenth and nineteenth centuries? Or was abundance in the form of free land, that is, an expanding frontier, more applicable during that period?

Another behaviorist approach is found in the selection by the English anthropologist, Geoffrey Gorer. Here the process of group character formation is approached by applying individual behavioral concepts to group behavioral patterns. Since groups are comprised of individuals it is possible to demonstrate the relationships that exist between individuals and the larger culture to which they belong. Gorer makes the analogy of the American revolt against English authority as a kind of psychological rejection of a father's authority. The cycle of rejection is seen first in the individual's emigration from the fatherland, and later in the revolt against the father's authority as he sought to adapt to accepted American behavioral patterns. Established in this way as a personality trait of first- and second-generation Americans, rejection of authority was repeatedly reinforced as a basic and persistent American character trait. While one may question Gorer's understanding and interpretation of the American Revolutionary period, the application of his approach to a historical problem is provocative. But does he answer the more fundamental question as to how these American values adopted by the second generation initially became different from European values?

Can ideas in the minds of men be as formative as actions and events? Were certain ideas or beliefs that were deeply rooted in the mass mind responsible for American behavior? Arthur A. Ekirch, Jr. argues in the next selection that the idea of *progress,* a philosophical abstraction in the salons of Europe, was translated by the common man in America into a pervasive sense of optimism and purpose. Essentially a part of European intellectual culture, the concept was "transmitted to and modified by the New World" where it was reshaped under the impact of the American environment. The confidence in the progress of the

American nation expressed by the Founding Fathers became, by the nineteenth century, a "dogma of widespread mass appeal." The apparent realization of progress, Ekirch argues, "served to strengthen the old idea that America enjoyed an especial and unique position in the world." The idea of progress thus became a dynamic reality to Americans and a basic force in the shaping of character. Ekirch does not believe, however, that ideas, such as progress, operate outside their environmental framework. It is not the idea purely, but the impact of the American environment upon the idea which gives it particular meaning in the American experience.

Oscar Handlin's second essay in this collection, while recognizing the influence of cultural traditions and institution and marked local variations in character, nevertheless sees an American nationality arising from a situation which required settlers searching for security and stability "constantly to seek out and to take risks." There was an open future of reward and plenty within the reach of all who shared the American situation. Thus Handlin argues that it is not similarities in "appearance, habits, manners or institutions" which gave Americans their sense of identity and nationality, but rather character traits that "came from the effort to maintain a balance between the longing for stability and the exposure to risks." Handlin sees this situation as a kind of cultural environment which molded the distinctive American character. But we still need to ask why these Americans did not accept security and reject the necessity for seeking out new risks and adventures.

A way out of this dilemma is suggested in the next selection. The American was as much affected by his hopes and expectations in a land that seemed to allow for mobility, change, and progress as he was affected by the limitations of past experience and the impact of physical conditions. Movement, Migration, Mobility—the M-Factor as George Wilson Pierson terms it—is a hybrid force which by a selective process has changed Europeans into Americans. Like David Potter's abundance thesis, the M-Factor thesis is highly inclusive, embracing both cultural and environmental influences. The Turner frontier hypothesis, for example, is extended and placed within a larger perspective. It is not the frontier *per se* which is important to Pierson, but the successive movements both *to* and *from* the frontier areas. But although Pierson places Turner's hypothesis in a larger framework, he rejects in part Potter's suggestion that the presence of abundant resources and a knowledge of technical skills required to exploit those resources was a basic element in the American experience. American beginnings, he holds, were difficult and required hard manual labor. Many of the regions that attracted the mobile settlers offered little actual abundance at the outset. Optimism, social equality, and democracy were character traits which grew not out of the condition of abundance, but rather were concomitants of the physical and social movements of the American people. Movement, to Pierson, means change, and the excessive mobility of Americans produced peculiar and lasting effects in the personalities and institutions of those who moved.

Do factors, such as those described in the third group of essays, which are largely nonexistent in an underdeveloped nation, have a more telling influence on character formation than either the cultural heritage or environment?

In reading each of the selections, the student must seek to find not the documentation of a single historical event, but rather broad patterns of activity and behavior shared by a significant portion of the inhabitants in an entire cultural area. In evaluating the essays in each section, one should question the ways in which the elements described are said to interact and should judge the extent to which each affected the formation of an American character.

The study of American culture and national character need not be considered a chauvinistic pursuit, for today, in a world where the American influence is felt in the most remote nations, it seems especially important that Americans and non-Americans understand more fully the conditions and motivations that have affected our national outlook, our policies, and our idealism. In this sense the study of American national cultural development seems essential to a sympathetic understanding of the problems and influences that shape the emerging nations.

In the reprinted selections footnotes appearing in the original sources have in general been omitted unless they contribute to the argument or better understanding of the selection.

THOMAS L. HARTSHORNE's (b. 1935) introductory chapter to his study of changing concepts of American character provides a useful and definitive primer to the student who would study this difficult and perplexing subject. The problems and misunderstandings related to national character study are pointed out, and a solid basis for historical generalization proposed.*

Thomas L. Hartshorne

An Introduction To National Character

It has become almost a national sport among American intellectuals to examine and criticize American life and institutions. Everything Americans do, everything foreigners say about us, is examined for the light it may shed on the American character. The American national character has become an American national obsession. Though I am concerned with the American character in this study, I make no attempt to describe, define, or explain that character. Rather, my goal is to determine what American intellectuals have offered in the way of descriptions, definitions, and explanations. My raw material, in other words, is not the national character itself, but the opinions people had and have about it.

Nor do I make an attempt to establish or to deny the theoretical validity of the concept of national character. The concept will be taken as given, and discussion and analysis should not be mistaken for either advocacy or condemnation. I do, however, have an opinion on the subject, and I feel I should state it in the interests of clarity. It seems to me that the concept of national character, especially when it is applied to a large, heterogeneous nation like the United States, is useful only as a large-scale generalization to cover the prominent characteristics of the national culture—not the traits of any supposedly typical individual personality. Thus, we may regard a particular collection of cultural traits as "typically American" if it is

*Thomas L. Hartshorne, *The Distorted Image: Changing Conceptions of the American Character Since Turner* (Cleveland: The Press of Case Western Reserve University, 1968), pp.ix–x, 1–9, 13–14. Most footnotes omitted.

exhibited more often or more intensely in America than in any other nation. In other words, the concept may prove useful as a semi-metaphorical descriptive device for a whole national culture, but it has no predictive value. One cannot with certainty assign an individual to any particular national group solely on the basis of his observed behavior, nor can one predict with any degree of accuracy how an individual member of a national group will behave in a given situation. The idea that there is such an animal as a "typical American" collapses under the weight of the enormous diversity of behavior exhibited by individual Americans. And what is true of Americans is equally true of Englishmen, Italians, Germans, Frenchmen, and members of any other nationality. . . .

The concept of national character seems to be one of those ideas that people find it almost impossible to do without. How often we find ourselves saying or thinking or hearing, "That's just like a Swede," or, "What else would you expect from a German?" We have even arrived at a sort of informal folkloric consensus concerning dominant national traits: Englishmen are staid, Germans militaristic, Frenchmen avaricious and amorous, Italians volatile, Spaniards haughty, the Japanese inscrutable, and so on. And there are many who insist, "There's just something about an American; you can always spot one in a foreign country."

Stated in this crude fashion, such attitudes make most intellectuals wince. Intellectuals are more likely than the average man is to be aware of the dangers of overhasty generalization, and while they might agree that it is possible in many cases to pick out American tourists in a foreign country, they would also insist that this is because they are tourists and not necessarily because they are Americans.

But intellectuals, too, come under the spell of the idea of national character. We find references to the idea in the works of historians, social scientists, literary critics—in fact, all those who study human behavior in any of its forms. It would appear that the concept of national character is the intellectual's substitute for the cruder practice of racial stereotyping.

The tendency has been with us for a long time. It is at least as old as the first relatively systematic attempts to understand human behavior and personality. When the ancient Greeks turned to the problem of observing and analyzing human behavior, the concept of group character found a place in their speculations. Hippocrates, Herodotus, and Aristotle, having observed their neighbors in the culturally crowded eastern Mediterranean area, came to the conclusion that their distinctive behavioral patterns had been produced by the particular geographic and climatic conditions under which they lived. Ever since these Greek thinkers turned to the analysis of people's behavior, countless others have followed their example; they have tried to isolate and describe distinctive behavioral uniformities among distinct groups of people and to determine what produced them.

All this despite the fact that warnings have been sounded against the practice. Boyd Shafer has argued that there is no such thing "as a constant or ever-present national character, unless it is invented by historians." But the fact remains that historians have been assiduous in their inventiveness, and there is no reason to suppose they will not continue to be. Max Weber went even further in asserting that "the appeal to national character is generally a mere confession of ignorance." He meant by this that the scholar who attempts to explain any individual's action on the basis of his nationality is not explaining anything at all. It may be perfectly true that individual X acted in a certain way because he was an inhabitant of country Y, and inhabitants of country Y always act that way, but there is more we need to know. It is a little like saying that the Green Bay Packers win championships because they win more football games than any other team in the National Football League; it tells us very little about the reasons for the Packers' success.

But the idea persists. Why? Because it is convenient. One of the jobs of the historian, or of any other analyst of human behavior, past or present, is to generalize on the basis of the available data, and the concept of national character may make his job easier. It is convenient to label large groups of people so they can be dealt with in a mass, ignoring for the moment their individual peculiarities. Such labels may facilitate thought and communication. But like all labels, the national-character label can be misused. People may forget that it is merely a label, a semantic convenience, that it ignores individual differences which may be significant in certain contexts; and they may begin to assume that it possesses some sort of intrinsic reality. At that point the label ceases to be an aid to thought and becomes a substitute for it.

Let us examine the assumptions implicit in the concept of national character.

Any collection of people which is not fortuitous and random is distinguished by certain characteristics that permit the ready identification of the group as a group. There is something about it that differentiates it from other groups; it is identifiable because it is distinctive in some way. Most of these distinctive characteristics consist of distinguishable patterns of behavior exhibited by members of the group. That is, groups are differentiated from one another because members of one act differently from members of another. And they act differently because they think or believe differently. Henry Pratt Fairchild points out that "it is the very essence of human association that persons who live together continuously in more or less intimate bonds of society should be characterized by many similarities of thought, feeling, and action." Ultimately, therefore, group differences exist because there are characterological differences between members of the group and those who are not members.

Of course, this reasoning could apply equally well to any human group. The concept of national character is a special case in which the group considered is the politically organized state. The analyst of national character tends to assume that the nation is the most important group to which the individual belongs; that it is his nation rather than his church, his political party, his occupational group, or his social class to which he owes his primary loyalty, which has the first claim on his services, and to which he will sacrifice his other loyalties in case there should be conflicts between them. In this view the nation is the primary locus of political, economic, and cultural influence upon the individual. It has, therefore, become the primary unit of interest for the historian and the social scientist. Because of this, the problem of national character as a special case of the larger problem of group character assumes a special importance.[1]

[1] It will be seen that there is a relationship between national character and nationalism, but that they are not by any means identical. To the extent that nationalism may be defined as the perception of differences between one's own national group and others, it may be said that the concept of national character is one manifestation of nationalistic thinking. On the other hand, nationalism usually connotes not only the perception of differences between one's own group and others but also a fervent belief in the superiority of one's own group. This is not true of the national-character study, which may just as easily be critical as commendatory.

These are the basic assumptions that lie behind the idea of national character. They are debatable at many points. To accept them wholeheartedly is to give assent to the proposition that in the ideal case there exists in any given group a personality type or a range of types so distinctive that it is possible to distinguish *each* member of the group from *all* nonmembers. This would appear to be impossible in practice. Even if we do not insist on full attainment of the ideal, we still find problems. Is it really possible to isolate for any particular group of people a set of "normal" behavior patterns that will serve to distinguish all members of the group from all non-members? It is always a distinct possibility that some members of the group may not exhibit the normal pattern and that some non-members may. In addition, the concept of "normality" itself implies some deviation. We are able to distinguish what is normal only because we are able to contrast it with the abnormal. Normality is essentially a statistical concept, an abstraction from many particular cases, and any particular case will probably only approximate the statistical norm. In other words, to speak of a range of normal behavior does not mean that all members of the group for which the norm has been deduced will exhibit the same behavioral patterns. For instance, murder is not a "normal" act in the cultures of Western Europe, but it does occur. The neat conceptualizations of social scientists often attain their neatness only by overlooking the fact that there are and always will be differences between individuals and that these differences may in certain instances be more obvious, and more important, than the similarities between the members of the group under examination at the moment.

Even if it were possible to isolate behavioral patterns in a group so that one could with absolute precision distinguish between members and non-members, it is not at all certain that these patterns would be reflections of underlying psychological uniformities. Two people may act in the same way in the same situation, but we cannot conclude that they are acting in the same way for the same reasons or that their acts have the same meanings for them. Nor is it possible to say that people who act differently do so because of personality differences. The task of deducing character or personality from observed behavior belongs to the psychologist and the psychiatrist, and it is difficult enough to do it for individuals without attempting to extend the process to large groups of people.

The study of national character involves all these difficulties and a few new ones besides. It requires the assumption that political citizenship creates psychological similarity. This is certainly a shaky assumption when applied to modern, heterogeneous nations which include people of many different occupations, religious beliefs, political views, class positions, and in many cases racial and linguistic backgrounds. Attempting to discover one national character to describe all these disparate elements would seem to be an impossible task. It would certainly run the risk of being far too abstract and generalized to provide an accurate picture of the more unusual types of people in the nation, the people who, precisely because of their deviation from the average, lend much of the distinctive color to the nation's life and culture. Indeed, national-character studies have been criticized on precisely these grounds: that they ignore too many of the differences that actually exist within the nation studied and present a picture that does violence to reality by being too uniform.

As if these theoretical difficulties implicit in the concept of national character were not enough, we also find at least one serious problem which is purely practical: no one seems to know precisely what the concept means. Or, if any author does have an idea, no one else agrees with him. Even the same author is likely to use the term in many different senses, and any two authors will probably have at least three different definitions—if they bother to define the phrase at all. Most do not, at least not explicitly, and many do not recognize that they are dealing with national character at all.

The phrase "American national character" may be used in two distinct senses: it may refer to the character of the individual American, or it may refer to the nation itself. The term "character" is interchangeably applicable to the nation and to the individual, and it may very well be used in both senses in the same work. It should be kept in mind, however, that this identity of usage is semantic only; the underlying realities are different. We may say, for instance, "Fluidity of class structure is an American characteristic." We may also say, "Aggressiveness is an American characteristic." The two statements refer to two different orders of phenomena, the first to America, the second to the American. The two conceptual models defined by Walter P. Metzger may be interpreted as special cases of these approaches. His "Freudian" model is a scheme for determining the personality of the individual; his "dramaturgical" model is a scheme for determining the cluster of social roles, norms, expectations, and values characteristic of a given society. The phrase "national character," therefore, is not always used in a sense which makes it identical with or analogous to individual character, nor does it necessarily mean individual character multiplied and writ large. It may have nothing whatever to do with individuals.

There are several other possible varieties of approach. The anthropologist Anthony F. C. Wallace has discussed some of the concepts which have been employed in the analysis of the relationship between the group and the personal characteristics of its members. He pointed out that this relationship could be described in the following ways: as the "genius" of a people, that is, the general frame of reference of the whole society; as the world view, the characteristic outlook of a people on the universe; as the "themes" of a particular culture, a list of propositions which describe the good life and the goals of human existence; as the "ethos," or usual style of emotional experience. To Wallace, national character was another concept of this kind, with its own unique features.

> The description of the national character of a people is apt to include statements about genius, world view, and values. What distinguishes national character as a concept is, first, its usual restriction to the citizens of modern, politically organized syates; and, second and more important, its emphasis upon the articulation of a large number of components into a structure or pattern.[2]

In addition, the personal background of the individual analyst of national character will affect his treatment. Anthropologists will tend to focus on kinship systems and child-rearing practices, psychologists on sibling rivalries and frustration-aggression complexes, sociologists on social structure, stratification patterns, and mobility, philosophers on dominant modes of thought and value systems. In short, the phrase "national character" has come

[2] *Culture and Personality* (New York, 1961), pp. 94–111.

to mean many different things, and the study of national character has come to involve the consideration of many different types of data with many different types of conceptual tools. To say that it is vague is a gross understatement. In practice the national-character study consists of a series of generalizations about a particular nation, designed to illustrate the ways in which it is distinctive.

Thus the difficulties in the way of the intelligent use of the concept of national character are serious, but they may be minimized if one clearly understands and constantly remembers that descriptions of national character are, and must be, descriptions of *tendencies* only. No conscientious student of national character would argue seriously that the inhabitants of any nation are uniform—psychologically or in any other respect. No one would attempt to prove that all Americans are alike. But a serious social scientist might argue that Americans tend to be more like each other than they are like the members of any other nation; that members of a given culture tend to respond in similar ways; that while there may be individual differences, the pressures of the culture will impose a more or less common direction on these individual differences and mitigate them to some extent; and that, since individuals are probably not that idiosyncratic inherently, there will emerge large areas of near uniformity. Kluckhohn and Murray have pointed out that every man is in some respects like all other men, in some respects like some other men, and in some respects like no other men. The analyst of national character works in the broad field covered by the second of these three propositions. He is concerned with the precise ways in which the individual member of a particular national culture is like the other members of that culture. By assuming the existence of a national character he has given tacit assent to the proposition that the individual constitutions of the people within the same national culture are nearly uniform in certain areas. And he has imposed upon himself the task of delineating these areas of near uniformity as precisely as he can.

This, however, presents another problem. The concept of national character is inherently comparative. When the analyst of American society reports, for example, that Americans are "joiners," he does not mean that all Americans join one or more voluntary organizations and that members of other national groups join no such organizations at all. What he means is that a greater proportion of Americans join such groups than is true in any other nation, or at least most other nations. In order to demonstrate the validity of such a generalization, the student of the American character would have to consider data from other nations as well as from the United States, but the fact is that most students of the American character have confined themselves to a consideration of data from the United States alone. . . .

Comparisons between American institutions and those of other nations or peoples are not always made explicit in the American-character study. In fact, usually there is no reference whatever to nations other than the United States. But behind this apparently exclusive concern with American institutions lie the need and the desire to understand and explain America so that it may be compared rationally to what is known and understood of other nations. The American-character study is thus a symptom of cultural self-consciousness, a manifestation of a feeling of ideological and cultural competition. Accordingly, the recent interest in the American character is nothing more than a particularly intense manifestation of a feeling and a response that have existed previously in American history.

There is another factor involved, a factor having to do not with great movements in history but with developments within the American intellectual community itself. In the early decades of the century, national character was defined as racial inheritance at least partly because many American intellectuals, enchanted by recent discoveries in biology, especially genetics, were avid in their desire to apply this new knowledge to an understanding of social phenomena, just as they had been swept off their feet shortly before by the possibilities that Darwinism seemed to offer in the study of human relations. The development of the culture concept by anthropologists and the increasing stature of Freudian psychiatry called the assumptions of the racists into question, and in the 1920's there emerged an explanation of national character on cultural and psychological principles. This shift, therefore, reflected a growing sociological sophistication among writers on the national character. This, in turn, was largely because the problem of national character was coming more and more to be treated as a problem in social science. Up to roughly 1930 most of the writers on the American character were philosophers, novelists, journalists, and literary critics. Beginning in the 1930's, however, sociologists, anthropologists, psychiatrists, and historians with a knowledge of other social sciences began to concern themselves with the problem. Investigation of the American character became a legitimate field of inquiry for the social scientist.

It still is. One of the more important trends in current research in the social sciences is the widespread attempt to develop inter-disciplinary cooperation. The study of national character lends itself admirably to the interdisciplinary approach; it is a difficult, if not impossible, undertaking if confined within the bounds of any single academic discipline. This is perhaps one of the reasons why academicians in general tended to shy away from the subject until recent times. With the current emphasis on interdisciplinary study the academician is not only permitted to indulge in the kind of broad generalization demanded by the subject of national character, but is even praised for doing it. Given the present state of development of the social sciences, analysis of the American character is precisely the kind of problem one would expect social scientists to investigate.

ALEXIS DE TOCQUEVILLE (1805–1859), most famous of the nineteenth-century European observers of American society, came to this country in 1831 on a mission to study American penal institutions. His study became in fact the much broader *Democracy in America,* published in 1835 and 1840. Tocqueville was one of the first observers to note systematically those character and institutional distinctions which made up American character and culture. Seeking a basic cause for these peculiarities, he saw the English cultural heritage as the most significant and pervasive influence upon the American character.*

Alexis de Tocqueville

Alexis de Tocqueville and America

After the birth of a human being his early years are obscurely spent in the toils or pleasures of childhood. As he grows up the world receives him, when his manhood begins, and he enters into contact with his fellows. He is then studied for the first time, and it is imagined that the germ of the vices and the virtues of his maturer years is then formed.

This, if I am not mistaken, is a great error. We must begin higher up; we must watch the infant in his mother's arms; we must see the first images which the external world casts upon the dark mirror of his mind; the first occurrences which he witnesses; we must hear the first words which awaken the sleeping powers of thought, and stand by his earliest efforts, if we would understand the prejudices, the habits, and the passions which will rule his life. The entire man is, so to speak, to be seen in the cradle of the child.

The growth of nations presents something analogous to this; they all bear some marks of their origin; and the circumstances which accompanied their birth and contributed to their rise, affect the whole term of their being.

If we were able to go back to the elements of states, and to examine the oldest monuments of their history, I doubt not that we should discover the primary cause of the prejudices, the habits, the ruling passions, and in short of all that constitutes what is called the national character: we should then find the expla-

*From Alexis de Tocqueville, *Democracy in America,* Henry Reeve, Trans., 2d American edition, (New York, 1838), pp. 9–15, 25–26. Footnotes omitted.

nation of certain customs which now seem at variance with prevailing manners, of such laws as conflict with established principles, and of such incoherent opinions as are here and there to be met with in society, like those fragments of broken chains which we sometimes see hanging from the vault of an edifice, and supporting nothing. This might explain the destinies of certain nations which seem borne along by an unknown force to ends of which they themselves are ignorant. But hitherto facts have been wanting to researches of this kind: the spirit of inquiry has only come upon communities in their latter days; and when they at length turned their attention to contemplate their origin, time had already obscured it, or ignorance and pride adorned it with truth-concealing fables.

America is the only country in which it has been possible to witness the natural and tranquil growth of society, and where the influence exercised on the future condition of states by their origin is clearly distinguishable.

At the period when the peoples of Europe landed in the New World, their national characteristics were already completely formed; each of them had a physiognomy of its own; and as they had already attained that stage of civilization at which men are led to study themselves, they have transmitted to us a faithful picture of their opinions, their manners, and their laws. The men of the sixteenth century are almost as well known to us as our contemporaries. America consequently exhibits in the broad light of day the phænomena which the ignorance or rudeness of earlier ages conceals from our researches. Near enough to the time when the states of America were founded to be accurately acquainted with their elements, and sufficiently removed from that period to judge of some of their results, the men of our own day seem destined to see further than their predecessors into the series of human events. Providence has given us a torch which our forefathers did not possess, and has allowed us to discern fundamental causes in the history of the world which the obscurity of the past concealed from them.

If we carefully examine the social and political state of America after having studied its history, we shall remain perfectly convinced that not an opinion, not a custom, not a law, I may even say not an event, is upon record which the origin of that people will not explain. The readers of this book will find the germ of all that is to follow in the present chapter, and the key to almost the whole work.

The emigrants who came at different periods to occupy the territory now covered by the American Union, differed from each other in many respects; their aim was not the same, and they governed themselves on different principles.

These men had, however, certain features in common, and they were all placed in an analogous situation. The tie of language is perhaps the strongest and the most durable that can unite mankind. All the emigrants spoke the same tongue; they were all offsets from the same people. Born in a country which had been agitated for centuries by the struggles of faction, and in which all parties had been obliged in their turn to place themselves under the protection of the laws, their political education had been perfected in this rude school, and they were more conversant with the notions of right, and the principles of true freedom, than the greater part of their European contemporaries. At the period of the first emigrations, the parish system, that fruitful germ of free institutions, was deeply rooted in the habits of the English; and with it the doctrine of the sovereignty of the people had been introduced even into the bosom of the monarchy of the House of Tudor.

The religious quarrels which have agitated the Christian world were then rife. England had plunged into the new order of things with headlong vehemence. The character of its inhabitants, which had always been sedate and reflecting, became argumentative and austere. General information had been increased by intellectual debate, and the mind had received a deeper cultivation. Whilst religion was the topic of discussion, the morals of the people were reformed. All these national features are more or less discoverable in the physiognomy of those adventurers who came to seek a new home on the opposite shores of the Atlantic.

Another remark, to which we shall hereafter have occasion to recur, is applicable not only to the English, but to the French, the Spaniards, and all the Europeans who successively established themselves in the New World. All these European colonies contained the elements, if not the development, of a complete democracy. Two causes led to this result. It may safely be advanced, that on leaving the mother-country the emigrants had in general no notion of superiority over one another. The happy and the powerful do not go into exile, and there are no surer guarantees of equality among men than poverty and misfortune. It happened, however, on several occasions that persons of rank were driven to America by political and religious quarrels. Laws were made to establish a gradation of ranks; but it was soon found that the soil of America was entirely opposed to a territorial aristocracy. To bring that refractory land into cultivation, the constant and interested exertions of the owner himself were necessary; and when the ground was prepared, its produce was found to be insufficient to enrich a master and a farmer at the same time. The land was then naturally broken up into small portions, which the proprietor cultivated for himself. Land is the basis of an aristocracy, which clings to the soil that supports it; for it is not by privileges alone, nor by birth, but by landed property handed down from generation to generation, that an aristocracy is constituted. A nation may present immense fortunes and extreme wretchedness; but unless those fortunes are territorial, there is no aristocracy, but simply the class of the rich and that of the poor.

All the British colonies had then a great degree of similarity at the epoch of their settlement. All of them, from their first beginning, seemed destined to witness the growth, not of the aristocratic liberty of their mother-country, but of that freedom of the middle and lower orders of which the history of the world has as yet furnished no complete example.

In this general uniformity several striking differences were however discernible, which it is necessary to point out. Two branches may be distinguished in the Anglo-American family which have hitherto grown up without entirely commingling; the one in the South, the other in the North.

Virginia received the first English colony; the emigrants took possession of it in 1607. The idea that mines of gold and silver are the sources of national wealth was at that time singularly prevalent in Europe; a fatal delusion, which has done more to impoverish the nations which adopted it, and has cost more lives in America, than the united influence of war and bad laws. The men sent to Virginia were seekers of gold, adventurers without resources and without character, whose turbulent and restless spirits endangered the infant colony, and rendered its progress uncertain. The artisans and agriculturists arrived afterwards; and although they were a more moral and orderly race of men, they were in nowise above the level of the inferior classes in England. No lofty conceptions, no intellectual system directed the foundation of these new settlements. The colony was scarcely established when slavery was introduced, and this was the main circumstance which has exercised so prodigious an influence on the character, the laws, and all the future prospects of the South.

Slavery, as we shall afterwards show, dishonors labor; it introduces idleness into society, and, with idleness, ignorance and pride, luxury and distress. It enervates the powers of the mind, and benumbs the activity of man. The influence of slavery, united to the English character, explains the manners and the social condition of the Southern States.

In the North, the same English foundation was modified by the most opposite shades of character; and here I may be allowed to enter into some details. The two or three main ideas which constitute the basis of the social theory of the United States were first combined in the Northern British colonies, more generally denominated the states of New England. The principles of New England spread at first to the neighboring states; they then passed successively to the more distant ones; and at length they imbued the whole Confederation. They now extend their influence beyond its limits over the whole American world. The civilization of New England has been like a beacon lit upon a hill, which after it has diffused its warmth around, tinges the distant horizon with its glow.

The foundation of New England was a novel spectacle, and all the circumstances attending it were singular and original. The large majority of colonies have been first inhabited either by men without education and without resources, driven by their poverty and their misconduct from the land which gave them birth, or by speculators and adventurers greedy of gain. Some settlements cannot even boast so honorable an origin; St. Domingo was founded by buccaneers; and, at the present day, the criminal courts of England supply the population of Australia.

The settlers who established themselves on the shores of New England all belonged to the more independent classes of their native country. Their union on the soil of America at once presented the singular phænomenon of a society containing neither lords nor common people, neither rich nor poor. These men possessed, in proportion to their number, a greater mass of intelligence than is to be found in any European nation of our own time. All, without a single exception, had received a good education, and many of them were known in Europe for their talents and their acquirements. The other colonies had been founded by adventurers without family; the emigrants of New England brought with them the best elements of order and morality, they landed in the desert accompanied by their wives and children. But what most especially distinguished them was the aim of their undertaking. They had not been obliged by necessity to leave their country, the social position they abandoned was one to be regretted, and their means of subsistence were certain. Nor did they cross the Atlantic to improve their situation or to increase their wealth; the call which summoned them from the comforts of their homes was purely intellectual; and in facing the inevitable sufferings of exile, their object was the triumph of an idea.

The emigrants, or, as they deservedly styled themselves, the Pilgrims, belonged to that English sect, the austerity of whose principles had acquired for them the name of Puritans. Puritanism was not merely a religious doctrine, but it corresponded in many points with the most absolute democratic and republican theories. It was this tendency which had aroused its most dangerous adversaries. Persecuted by the Government of the mother-country, and disgusted by the habits of a society opposed to the rigor of their own principles, the Puritans went forth to seek some rude and unfrequented part of the world, where they could live according to their own opinions, and worship God in freedom. . . .

The remarks I have made will suffice to display the character of Anglo-American civilization in its true light. It is the result (and this should be constantly present to the mind) of two distinct elements, which in other places have been in frequent hostility, but which in America have been admirably incorporated and combined with one another. I allude to the spirit of Religion and the spirit of Liberty.

The settlers of New England were at the same time ardent sectarians and daring innovators. Narrow as the limits of some of their religious opinions were, they were entirely free from political prejudices.

Hence arose two tendencies, distinct but not opposite, which are constantly discernible in the manners as well as in the laws of the country.

It might be imagined that men who sacrificed their friends, their family, and their native land to a religious conviction, were absorbed in the pursuit of the intellectual advantages which they purchased at so dear a rate. The energy, however, with which they strove for the acquirements of wealth, moral enjoyment, and the comforts as well as liberties of the world, is scarcely inferior to that with which they devoted themselves to heaven.

Political principles, and all human laws and institutions were moulded and altered at their pleasure; the barriers of the society in which they were born were broken down before them; the old principles which had governed the world for ages were no more; a path without a term, and a field without an horizon were opened to the exploring and ardent curiosity of man: but at the limits of the political world he checks his researches, he discreetly lays aside the use of his most formidable faculties, he no longer consents to doubt or to innovate, but carefully abstaining from raising the curtain of the sanctuary, he yields with submissive respect to truths which he will not discuss.

Thus in the moral world, everything is classed, adapted, decided and foreseen; in the political world everything is agitated, uncertain, and disputed: in the one is a passive, though a voluntary, obedience: in the other an independence, scornful of experience and jealous of authority.

These two tendencies, apparently so discrepant, are far from conflicting; they advance together, and mutually support each other.

Religion perceives that civil liberty affords a noble exercise to the faculties of man, and that the political world is a field prepared by the Creator for the efforts of the intelligence. Contented with the freedom and the power which it enjoys in its own sphere, and with the place which it occupies, the empire of religion is never more surely established than when it reigns in the hearts of men unsupported by aught beside its native strength.

Religion is no less the companion of liberty in all its battles and its triumphs; the cradle of its infancy, and the divine source of its claims. The safe-guard of morality is religion, and morality is the best security of law as well as the surest pledge of freedom.

EDWARD EGGLESTON (1837–1902), best known as writer of the popular novel, *The Hoosier Schoolmaster,* was also a social and cultural historian and one of the founders of the American Historical Association. His *The Transit of Civilization from England to America in the Seventeenth Century,* first published in 1900, marked a significant departure in American historiography. Dealing primarily with the "mental furniture which the early English emigrants carried aboard ship with them," the study seeks the basis for what Eggleston called "Anglo-Saxon culture in America." By a consideration of many social and cultural topics, such as education, religion, and domestic life, Eggleston pointed the way to a "history of culture, the real history of men and women."*

Edward Eggleston

The Mental Furniture of Immigrants

What are loosely spoken of as national characteristics are probably a result not so much of heredity as of controlling traditions. Seminal ideas received in childhood, standards of feeling and thinking and living handed down from one overlapping generation to another, make the man English or French or German in the rudimentary outfit of his mind. A gradual change in fundamental notions produces the difference between the character of a nation at an early epoch and that of the same people in a later age. In taking account of the mental furniture which the early English emigrants carried aboard ship with them, we shall gain a knowledge of what may be called the original investment from which has been developed Anglo-Saxon culture in America. The mother country of the United States was England in the first half of the seventeenth century, or, at most, England before the Revolution of 1688. From the English spoken in the days of the Stuart kings came our primitive speech, and the opinions, prejudices, and modes of thinking of the English in that day lay at the bottom of what intellectual life there was in the colonies. Some seventeenth-century characteristics, long since lost or obscured in England, may yet be recognized in the folk-lore and folk-speech, the superstitions and beliefs of people in America. The number of English who crossed the seas before the middle of the century

*From Edward Eggleston, *The Transit of Civilization from England to America in the Seventeenth Century* (Boston, 1900), pp. 1–3.

was above thirty thousand. Those who survived the first rude outset of pioneer life, with their fast-multiplying progeny, numbered probably fifty thousand in 1650, and this population was about halved between the colonies on the Chesapeake waters and those to the northward of the Dutch settlement on the New England coast. To these early comers it is due that the speech, the usages, the institutions, and the binding traditions of the United States are English.

In reckoning the mental outfit of the first comers we should only mislead ourselves by recalling the names of Jonson and Shakespeare and the other lights that were shining when the Susan Constant and her two little consorts sailed out of the Thames to bear a company of English people to the James River. Nor will it avail much to remember that Milton was a Puritan at the same time with Cotton and Hooker and Winthrop. The emigrants had no considerable part in the higher intellectual life of the age; the great artistic passions of Shakespeare and Milton touched them not at any point. Bacon's contribution to the art of finding truth did not belong to them. Men may live in the same time without being intellectual contemporaries.

The medieval dissenting tradition of English culture which predates the English reformation is seen by THOMAS CUMING HALL (1858–1936), former Professor at Union Theological Seminary, as the underlying basis for American character. The belief that the individual could interpret scripture and seek his own salvation without the agency of an historic church or clergy gave rise to a world view which deeply influenced behavioral patterns in all aspects of American life.*

Thomas Cuming Hall

The English Dissenting Tradition

American history begins before America was discovered. The United States are what they are because men from England carried with them to the new land a strong tradition born of long struggle with what they thought or instinctively felt were strange and un-English ways.

The story of that tradition, especially upon its religious side, has been so misread or neglected that whole chapters of North American history are even now crying for rewriting.

A creative tradition cannot be reduced to any one simple formula. The interests of human life are too complicated to be enclosed in a phrase, and although the economic interpretation of history has thrown a flood of light upon many dark places in the study of the forms that religion, law and politics take, the word economic must be very broadly interpreted and made to include nearly all human wants and urges, in order to greatly help us. And amongst the most constant historic urges is one that is perhaps not capable of complete definition, but which under many several forms we call religion.

It is strange that in all that has been written about the United States in recent years little has been said about our religious history. We have many books more or less satisfactory about our economic history; our civilization has been well and fully treated in many books; our politics, our social structure and our literature

*From Thomas Cuming Hall, *The Religious Background of American Culture* (New York: Frederick Ungar Publishing Company, Inc., 1930, 1959), pp. vii–xii. Footnotes omitted.

have been amply dealt with; but an attempt to trace the course of our religious history seems to be utterly lacking. . . .

This is the more surprising, because the early historians like George Bancroft and Palfrey have dealt with the history of New England as if it were the story of a religious experiment pure and simple, which it certainly was not. The thoughtful student of the religious streams of feeling recurrent in our history will find in them some explanation of many of our present most pressing questions. We will attempt to outline in a purely impartial way some of these currents and explain their connection with our advancing life. We take no attitude in regard to the truth or untruth of the religious positions examined; that is a personal judgment of worth with which in these pages we have no concern. We only insist that an examination of these currents and tides of religious thought and feeling cannot be passed by, without serious misinterpretation of American life.

To understand certain phases of life in America, whether on Fifth Avenue in New York or the Lake Shore Drive in Chicago, one must go back to the mists and half-lights of the days of King Edward III in England. The study therefore of the English dissenting tradition should be the first step in trying to understand the American Republic, and this fact has been forgotten or never realized; hence the story of our relations to England has often been clouded and rendered hazy and unsatisifactory. It is neither helpful nor accurate to constantly speak of our English tradition without at once asking which of several English traditions we really mean. For English life is not and never has been dominated by only one tradition, no matter how much of a unit the nation may at times seem to have been. And it is the business of the thoughtful historian to ask himself which English tradition is really fundamental in American life.

In spite of our very conglomerate population, it is confessedly an English tradition that governs the life of the American Republic, and which has given us our speech. French, Spanish, Dutch, Scandinavian and other elements, not to speak of the Irish and Scotch, have built themselves into the fabric of a common American life, but none of the fifty-two non-American varieties of national groups mentioned in the Inter-Church Commission's Report on the steel strike of 1919 has had the numbers, unity and cohesion sufficient to seriously challenge the supremacy of the Anglo-Saxon in North America. Although probably from sixty to seventy per cent of the population has non-English blood in its veins, no other national unit has been able to force either its speech or its tradition on even a small area of the United States. And as a governing class rose in the colonies, it was able to absorb even hostile elements and mold them to a common will as, for instance, in Manhattan and New Jersey.

It must then be of deepest interest to ask what is this tradition; where lies the power it possesses; where and when did it arise; and what is its main content?

We hope to show that the answer of the schoolbooks and the newspapers, which is generally that it is the Puritan tradition, is both superficial and unhistorical. We will try to demonstrate that Puritanism properly understood has very little to do with marking our mentality or giving modes and patterns to our thought.

At the most English Puritanism only affected one region and that for only a very short time. We hope to prove that the real type of thought and feeling which has guided and guarded the onward march of American civilization is much older, stronger and broader in its reach than English Puritanism ever was. For the foundation of the American social structure is, we hope to show, the much older dissenting tradition of England; and that to understand our history we must free ourselves from many prejudices and cease to speak by rote the familiar phrases of the history books, and study anew the character and content of English Dissent.

We are not writing for the theological specialist, and will therefore very briefly point out what our main contention will be. We hope to show that an old, radical and hardy English Protestantism existed before the Continental type of Protestantism appeared, and that it is this radical Protestantism that has dominated and to a great extent still dominates Anglo-American thinking.

Roughly we may divide Christian groups for our purposes on the basis of their estimate of the highest authority in religion. The Roman Catholic Church believes in a living organic Church as the highest authority, with the Holy Father as its infallible mouthpiece when he speaks officially *"ex cathedra."* The Anglo-Catholic group regards the national Church as an authoritative living organization, with an historic episcopate reaching back to the Founder of the Christian Church to guarantee the validity of orders and sacraments and the purity of the faith. The Continental type of Protestantism regards the Word of God contained in the Scriptures of the Old and New Testament as the highest authority, but looks to a pure conciliar historic Church to interpret that Word. This pure Church is easily recognized by its possession of an orderly ministry, sacraments rightly administered and a pure churchly discipline adequately maintained. The old English radical Protestantism, under the stress of persecution, poverty and cultural isolation, broke with the thought of an authoritative and interpreting Church, as well as with the conception of a priestly ministry and laid the emphasis solely upon the Bible as God's Word and as sufficient for salvation to every believing soul. Every individual was capable of being led of the Spirit to a right understanding of Scripture, and needed no historic Church and no priesthood to guide and interpret.

As a matter of fact, the thought of this old dissenting Protestantism was deeply affected by historic Christianity without always knowing whence its conceptions arose. For instance, the stern predestinarianism of Paul, Augustine and Wyclif became a common characteristic of Dissent, but so little did it know of its origin, indeed so little does it still know of it, that this is nearly always attributed to Calvin, often where Calvin was utterly unknown, or where, had he been known, he would have been regarded with deep suspicion because of his High Churchism and deeply sacramental character.

All this we hope to set forth more elaborately and yet in terms all may understand; and hope that all who read and understand will in the future instinctively translate the term "Puritan" in ninety-nine cases out of a hundred by the more exact phrase, "the Anglo-American Dissenting Mind."

DIXON RYAN FOX (1887–1945) was for many years Professor of History at Columbia University, climaxing his career as President of Union College. His concern with shifting cultural patterns was expressed in his book *The Decline of Aristocracy in the Politics of New York: 1801–1840* (1919). In the important essay reprinted here, Fox illustrates how, in a number of specific professional areas, the cultural practices of England and Europe were transplanted rapidly to the successive frontiers of American settlement, enabling the high culture of the past to be preserved.*

Dixon Ryan Fox

The Transplantation of Culture to America

Civilization in Transit[1]

A quarter of a century ago Edward Eggleston published a volume whose title set the reader thinking before he turned the cover, *The Transit of Civilization from England to America in the Seventeenth Century*. Americans, then, did not invent their culture, but had to bring its elements from Europe bit by bit, however much they might be modified by transplantation. The thoughtful reader, setting side by side before his mind's eye a picture of the shaggy wilderness the colonists had to conquer and that of the age-old communities they had left behind, might readily presume that, though the individuals were hardly conscious of it, the process which the book would trace was neither short nor simple. What Eggleston considered was not the fundamental economic problem of staying alive in a new country, but the saving and carrying forward of arts and sciences, those refinements and specializations which come from intelligently living together. The transit, quite obviously, was not completed in the seventeenth century, nor is it yet complete; and when a given institution or practice reached the western shores of the Atlantic it yet had far to go. Few men could have realized this more vividly than Eggleston himself, who had spent the years of his young-manhood as

[1] This paper was read before the meeting of the American Historical Association at Rochester, Dec. 29, 1926.

*From Dixon Ryan Fox, "Civilization in Transit," *American Historical Review*, XXXII, pp. 753–768. By permission of the American Historical Association.

a circuit rider in southern Indiana and the farther West and been a herald and exemplar of civilization in the backwoods.

Much has been written of the man with the axe, slowly cutting back the forest, fighting off malaria and mortgages as well as wild beasts and Indians and horse-thieves and establishing American ideals of energy and self-reliance. These men and women of the cabin did the basic work; they cleared the way and built foundations. At the beginning of the nineteenth century they constituted more than nine-tenths of our population. But if all had been of this type who made their way across the sea and across American hills and valleys it would have taken many centuries to build a great civilization. In their wake followed pioneers of ideas and special competence, quite as brave and worthy. As the woodsman-farmer with his axe and hoe took a risk, whether untamed nature would let him live, so these men with the book, the scalpel, the compass, to say nothing of the microscope and test-tube, took a risk, whether the social soil was deep and rich enough to sustain their specialties. How professional competence was transplanted to America makes an interesting study.

Let us begin with a well-known figure, the family doctor. The herbalists and leeches who came over during the first century were certainly not highly skilled, even when they made healing the sick their chief concern and not merely a sideline of the Christian ministry. But their obvious usefulness at last stirred certain native youth to equal or surpass them, not through mere apprenticeship but by resort to the original sources of instruction in Europe. In 1734 young William Bull, of Charles Town, returned with his M.D. from the University of Leyden, and six years later Isaac Dubois, of New York, could claim the same distinction; during the thirty-five years that followed scores of young men undertook the arduous journey with the same ambition, most of them taking up their study in Edinburgh. Two so graduated, Drs. William Shippen and John Morgan, returned to Philadelphia in the seventeen-sixties prepared to set up formal courses of instruction. "The time was ripe," and from their efforts grew the medical school of that city, soon rivalled by a second at King's College in New York. In both cases the staff was largely of British training and the methods closely imitative, even to the printed doctor's thesis, oftentimes in Latin, solemnly defended before the assembled faculty. In time it was loudly boasted, and finally believed, that one might become a first-rate doctor without going to Europe, and by the early years of the nineteenth century these and other medical schools were staffed with their own product. It had taken about two centuries to transfer medical science to America.

The major phenomena of the transit are well illustrated by this type example. Four stages are discerned: first, when foreign practitioners of the specialty are received by the pioneer community; second, when the native youth go to the old country to attend upon instruction; third, when institutions of the special learning are established in the new land, though still dependent on the metropolis for the equipment of their teachers; fourth, when the institutions have sufficiently developed to maintain themselves.

He who applies this key to others of the older professional specialties will be surprised to see how well it works. It enables us to see the present stage of transit in various concerns. In great music we are still to a considerable degree in the first stage—so obviously true is this that certain *virtuosi* sprung from old American village stock, like Mme. Nordica and Ricardo Martin, have thought it added to their personal prestige to Europeanize their names. In pictorial and plastic art we are emerging from the second stage into the third. In university scholarship we reached the fourth stage only at the end of the last century; it was not long ago that a German Ph.D. was deemed essential to a first-class professor. In dentistry we have *reversed* the process to the third stage; in architecture, in some forms of applied science, and perhaps in business organization, we have reversed it to the second. After these reflections we may, perhaps, propose a generalization applicable to the normal conditions of modern history: professional competence rises through provincial to metropolitan status by the process of reception, attendance, dependent organization, and self-maintenance. If we were to stifle our sense of humor we might even call this a "law." At least it has the two major requisites of a sociological law, in that when baldly stated it is so ponderously cryptic as to be unintelligible, and when explained it is so obvious that it need not have been stated at all.

It must be understood that in this use of the word "provincial" there is no reference of necessity to political dependence. Metropolis and province may change places without regard to politics; ideas flowed from France into England in the Norman days, and from England into France during the first half of the eighteenth century. Sometimes, indeed, the victors adopt the culture of their victims, as when in the phrase of Horace:

> Greece, conquered Greece, her conquerors
> subdued
> And clownish Latium with her arts imbued.

The importation of culture has oftentimes been artificially stimulated by autocrats—assumption by fiat—as is recalled by mention of the names of Peter the Great and Mustapha Kemal, to say nothing of the ministers of Mutsuhito. And the export has been stimulated quite as well. Christian missions have been a most important agency in carrying secular culture abroad as well as religious, if, indeed, the two can be sharply distinguished. Many patriotic Frenchmen, for example, who believe the Catholic faith a silly superstition contribute to its propagation beyond the seas, proud that "backward areas" are thus becoming Gallicized. Publications of hyphenate societies supported at least in part from the old homeland abound in many places. But the process has worked normally without artificial aid. Cataclysms may stimulate it, as when in the seventeen-nineties the *émigrés* from France and Santo Domingo brought French opera, cotillions, and fine cooking to America. Dr. Samuel Latham Mitchill, in a discourse delivered in 1821, declared that European wars had been the cause of a quickened transit of books from the Old World to the New, that some distinguished refugees had brought their libraries, that booksellers, deprived of markets at home, had brought their stocks in increasing number: "The storm from the east has wafted, in short, an abundance of precious things to these regions." But, again, the process can not be generally explained as a concomitant of great disturbance in the metropolis.

The operation in particulars, indeed, seems strikingly accidental, and this not only in the professions but in the trades as well, where, of course, the first stage merges directly into the last. Naturalists tell us that in the islands of the South Sea the wind and flying birds carry spores and seeds from one land-area to another, where if the soil conditions are propitious a plant springs up and a part of the flora is thus reproduced beyond the water. Almost as fortuitous seem the circumstances by which carriers of civilization have been transferred to America.

Take, for example, the case of Samuel Slater, in 1789 an apprentice spinner in the employ of Richard Arkwright's partner in Belper, England. Learning by chance at the age of twenty-one, when his term of service had expired, that there was some curiosity in America as to Arkwright's patents, he resolved to try his fortune overseas. But the statute of 22, George III, chapter 60, framed according to old mercantilist doctrine, forbade the taking out of England of any machinery, models, or mechanical drawings and, indeed, the migration of artisans. So young Slater by a feat of concentration memorized the entire series of wheels and bands and rollers with precise dimensions and, disguised as a countryman, slipped by the English customs officers without their once suspecting the illicit cargo that he carried in his mind. On arriving in New York he heard that Moses Brown, a Rhode Island Quaker, had made some trials at cotton spinning, and wrote him a letter setting forth what he could do. The answer came quite promptly: "If thee canst do this thing, I invite thee to come to Rhode Island, and have the credit of introducing cotton manufacture into America." Thereupon he went to Pawtucket, the one most fortunate place in the country, where waterwheels and ships were found within the same small town, and there he built his frames and did become what Moses Brown had prophesied. The seed had landed on good soil.

It is somewhat puzzling to the reader of industrial statistics to account for the concentration of the brass manufacture in the Naugatuck Valley in Connecticut. There is neither copper, nor zinc, nor coal found in that vicinity, nor is it exceptionally well placed for transportation; why, then, should eighty-five per cent of America's brass be made there? The answer is, the accident of the carrier. In 1820 an artisan named Crofts left a Birmingham brass-works as an emigrant. On landing in America he drifted about and finally into Waterbury. Here he found some humble manufacturers making notions for tin-peddlers, among other things a few brass buttons from old copper kettles and ship bottoms and imported zinc. Hiring out as a hand he showed his new employers better methods, was made a partner, and was sent back to Birmingham some seven or eight times to recruit more skilled workers; on the basis of this skill the brass business was established.

If one works through the records of any branch of human effort in America, one comes upon these carriers, individual men and women more or less conscious of the function they perform. In 1805 one Ferdinand Rudolph Hassler came from Switzerland to Philadelphia, bringing with him some books and mathematical instruments. Through the good offices of Secretary Gallatin, his compatriot, and the interest of President Jefferson, he was given a place as a teacher at West Point, and thus brought the knowledge of analytical geometry to America; he advised the government as to a method of charting the coastal waters, was sent abroad to buy more instruments, and on his return began the United States Coast Survey. The man with the special competence had happened to meet the special need. About the same time, in 1816, there came to the military academy Claude Crozet, who had been schooled at the Polytechnique in Paris—and thus began the study of descriptive geometry in this country; having been an engineer under Napoleon and having had the severe training in higher mathematics that most of our practitioners sadly lacked, after seven years' teaching he became an employee of Virginia and gave the state a system of roads which made it for that time a model.

This was the contribution of two Europeans to American mathematics. English books were usually the seeds of early American architecture, but there were human carriers too, that we can recognize, like Richard Upjohn, who in 1829 brought to New England the ideas of the Gothic revival, later to flower in his Trinity Church in New York City. Similar stories could be told for almost every branch of art and science.

But some have transferred to the province parts of the metropolitan environment itself. In 1714 the ablest young thinkers of Connecticut were spinning out dry dichotomies of dry ideas—working knowledge out of their own heads, as the Reverend Samuel Johnson wrote in reminiscence. Then there came to Yale a library which Jeremy Dummer, the colonial agent, had sent from the old country, and for the first time New England came into contact with John Locke and Isaac Newton and modern thought. The effect, as Johnson writes of it, was sudden and tremendous; he himself and other clergymen left Calvinism and stirred the religious thinking of the Puritan colonies as it had not been stirred before—all because of a library. In 1796, or thereabouts, Dr. Adam Seybert, of Philadelphia, brought back from Europe a cabinet of minerals, the second in the country; it was to this collection that young Benjamin Silliman, of New Haven, brought a little box of stones for comparison and identification, and thus was started on his way to be the first great American master of geology, and it was the elaborate cabinet which Colonel George Gibbs brought across the water that aided Silliman to make Yale the centre of such studies. In 1794 Dr. David Hosack returned with a duplicate collection of plants from the herbarium of Linnaeus, and shortly afterward brought in seeds, slips, and shrubs to form his botanical garden, specimens from which made up the core of the great establishment in Bronx Park; such new advantages made the study of botany by Americans a very different thing from what it had been before.

The fine art of Europe was started westward only when American wealth had sufficiently accumulated to secure it. There were collections as early as the seventeen-nineties, like that brought to Boston by James Swan, and that to Philadelphia by William Hamilton, but they had little cultural value while shut within a few private houses. It was not until the latter half of the nineteenth century, about 1870, to be exact, that private fortune seriously took up the task of educating the public taste by transferring European art to open galleries in this country. Notable collections of Italian primitives and other pieces were given to the New York Historical Society by Thomas Jefferson Bryan and to Yale by James J. Jarves; William W. Corcoran in 1869 endowed a museum in Washington to receive his importations; in 1870 one group of philanthropists organized the Museum of Fine Arts in Boston and another the Metropolitan Museum in New York City. Such benefactions though conspicuous for scale were not different in spirit from earlier and more modest transfers like that accomplished by Daniel Wadsworth and his associates for Hartford in 1842 and that by the Reverend A. W. Freeman who brought copies to the Indiana colleges in the sixties and seventies. By reason of such establishments artists could see something of the legacy of bygone centuries without leaving their own soil. The process was continued by Morgan, Frick, and a host of others, until now, apparently, American purchasers are so much the reliance of those who market the historic art of Europe that collections, like that of Lord Leverhulme, are moved here intact for the auctioneer. Thus, in the transit of civilization one factor has been the removal of environment itself.

The transit as a whole, apparently, was speeded by the Revolution, which for a time so developed the sentiment of nationalism that it irked us to depend on Europe for anything. The audience at the John Street Theatre, New York, on April 16, 1787, applauded the prologue of Royall Tyler's play, *The Contrast,* with its announcement of an innovation:

> Exult each patriot heart—tonight is shewn
> A piece which we may fairly call our own;
> Where the proud titles of "My Lord! Your Grace!"
> To humble Mr. and plain Sir give place.
> Our author pictures not from foreign climes
> The fashions or the follies of the times;
> But has confin'd the subject of his work
> To the gay scenes—the circles of New York.

In the introduction to her novel *Dorval, the Speculator* (1801), Madam Wood, of Portland, echoed the same sentiment: "Hitherto we have been indebted to France, Germany, and Great Britain, for the majority of our literary pleasures. Why we should not aim at independence, with respect to our mental enjoyments, as well as our more substantial gratifications, I know not. Why must the amusements of our leisure hours cross the Atlantic? . . . The following pages are wholly American; the characters are those of our own country."

The customary deference and dependence, it is true, were not easily thrown off. In colonial days many whose ancestors had lived here for a hundred years and who themselves had never left our shores still spoke wistfully of England as "home." William Dunlap, the leading theatrical manager at the beginning of the nineteenth century, was not a little irritated by the general distrust of American playwrights; *The Contrast* itself was none too successful. The New York *Columbian,* praising a new play in 1819, was impressed with its own courage: "We advance this opinion without waiting for the fiat of an English audience, or an English review." Fenimore Cooper, the following year, did not dare confess the American authorship of his first novel and sent it out more safely as the work of an anonymous Englishwoman. The highest encomium his later admirers could pronounce was to call him the American Scott; many, however, thought this hardly in good taste, not because it indicated undue deference to British standards, but because the comparison seemed presumptuous. Nevertheless, the national consciousness was coming. Most Americans were extremely sensitive when British critics dismissed us as provincial. The bitter vehemence of C. J. Ingersoll, Robert Walsh, and Paulding, who tried to prove that we were not, was perhaps in itself a telling bit of evidence that we still were; but, for all that, there was a growing sentiment that it was time for Americans, even in concerns outside of government, to assume "the separate and equal station to which the Laws of Nature and of Nature's God entitled them."

The science of botany gives an interesting example. Since it did not reach the status of a specialized profession in Europe until far on in the nineteenth century, it can not well be subjected to our "law." Yet it had an interesting process of its own in transition. First came European explorers, like Mark Catesby and Peter Kalm; then, somewhat overlapping, Americans who were the correspondents of great scholars in the old countries, such as John Clayton, who sent collections to Gronovius, and John Bartram, who supplied the English Quaker, Peter Collinson. But the amateur botanists of the United States, mostly doctors of medicine or of divinity, resented foreign domination, especially such European christening of American plants. "We ought," wrote the most distinguished of them, the Reverend H. E. Muhlenberg, in 1811, "we ought to be jealous for our American names. Why should we have the trouble of finding, and other nations the honor?" In this concern, as in many others, patriotism spurred us to catch up with Europe. Sometimes the cultural self-reliance was encouraged by the old country; the American Board of Commissioners for Foreign Missions (1810) and the American Bible Society (1816) were formed because English organizations not unnaturally refused to undertake the administration of American philanthropy. But generally the new nation insisted on becoming as free as possible in every way.

Every circumstance that favored this great enterprise was heartily welcomed. Every discovery of materials in America —of some mineral useful in the arts, some root or bark that could contribute to our pharmacopoeia—was hailed as an amendment to the Declaration of Independence. When in 1810 the first trained veterinary surgeon landed in New York, Americans expressed their gratification that the transit of that science had begun; the naturalization of merino sheep was applauded like a victory on the battle-field. When in 1807 Joel Barlow's epic poem was published in Philadelphia, patriots deplored that it had been found necessary to make the illustrations in England, while the first volume of Alexander Wilson's handsome *Ornithology* was welcomed the following year with special satisfaction because in type, ink, paper, engraving, and binding it was American—everything except the reds and blues used in the coloring of the birds, which had to come from France. But we were not to be made free from European skill as promptly as we thought. There is now nearing completion the sumptuous six-volume work of Mr. I. N. Phelps Stokes, *The Iconography of Manhattan Island,* which traces the physical growth of New York City, or at least its principal borough, during the three hundred years since its foundation by the Dutch. It is a striking circumstance that much of the paper and the fine engraving has had to be imported from Holland. New York is, then, in some slight degree, still New Netherland.

Our emancipation has indeed been gradual, every step painfully worked out. In our texts of learning we have risen slowly from Noah Webster's spelling book, which supplanted the English Dilworth, to the latest American treatise for advanced collegiate study; our first college text-book in economics was a mere adaptation of the Scottish McCulloch; our American texts in the classics were slightly rearranged from European editions; our greatest achievement in mathematics up to 1830 was Bowditch's translation of Laplace. In 1894 Professor Florian Cajori published a general history of mathematics. The reader notices that he mentions but few Americans—none until the eighteen-seventies, the time of Benjamin Pierce. The patriotic American in his chagrin ascribes this omission to ignorance of what had been achieved on this side of the Atlantic; then he finds that the professor had four years before published a history of mathematics in the United States, a book of four hundred pages. He who well knew the contribution of America in this branch of higher learning could see, when called upon to take the broad view, how negligible it was.

In chemistry, physics, and other fields, despite the rapid strides of recent years, the story is still much the same. In the list of winners of the Nobel Prize for research in pure science America does not figure brightly. It is the office of our Department of Commerce to watch our national expenditures; in a recent address Secretary Hoover pointed out that we are spending ten times as much for cosmetics as for advancing scientific knowledge. This is not true, he observes, of older civilizations. We still have much to learn from Europe; the transit of civilization to America is by no means complete.

Let us turn, however, to follow it from the Atlantic shore. To illustrate our law of transit let us look for a moment at the South. In the colonial period it was more truly a cultural province than the North, which was well advanced in the third stage when the South was in the middle of the second. The Revolution cut it off somewhat from the metropolis across the water and it became a cultural province of the North. First, there were young Northerners who went South to practise their professions, like Abraham Baldwin, the Connecticut lawyer, who is called the "Father of the University of Georgia." The New England Society of Charleston, formed in 1819, had prominent professional men upon its rolls. There were many in later times who thus went South to teach, men like Eli Whitney, William H. Seward, William Ellery Channing, Sergeant S. Prentiss, Amos Kendall, and Jared Sparks. Overlapping with this stage, the Southerners began in much greater number to send their sons to college in the North, and in the early decades of the nineteenth century from ten to thirty per cent of the attendance at Yale and Princeton was from that section. M. Moreau de Saint Méry, visiting the latter college in 1794, remarked the surprising number of young men from Virginia and the Carolinas. In the professions the tendency was even more impressive; for a long time Georgia led the states outside Connecticut in attendance at the Litchfield Law School, with South Carolina as a close competitor; about half the students at the medical school of the University of Pennsylvania were from the South. When news of the Richmond Theatre fire of 1811 reached Philadelphia, scores of Virginians then enrolled—one incredulous reporter said more than a hundred—met to listen to a memorial sermon.

Meanwhile the third stage had begun. Many collegiate institutions were established, but they were staffed by men of Northern training. In 1804, the president of the University of Georgia was Josiah Meigs, of Middletown, Connecticut, who had studied at Yale and taught there; the president of the College of South Carolina was Jonathan Maxcy, of Attleborough, Massachusetts, who had studied at Brown and taught there; the president of the University of North Carolina was Joseph Caldwell, of Lammington, New Jersey, who had studied at Princeton and taught there. The upland colleges were most of them heavily indebted to Princeton. Jefferson, who contemplated importing directly the whole faculty of the University of Geneva for his institution in Charlottesville, was an exception. Up to 1830, at least, the South was a cultural province of the North. Then came the explosions that began the rift between the sections—the abolition movement, the ominous slave rebellion, the tariff controversy, Webster's reply to Hayne; the South became painfully self-conscious, declared her cultural independence and developed a literature of her own. It will be remembered that J. P. Kennedy's *Swallow Barn,* the South's first novel of importance, appeared in 1832, Poe's first story in 1833, Simms's *Guy Rivers* in 1834, and the *Southern Literary Messenger* in 1835.

The seaboard South, when political independence was achieved, was a settled country and a fairly well-defined geographical area. But "the West" throughout American history, until recently, has been a relative term, a phenomenon of movement, a degree of settlement; what was the west of one generation was the east of the next, when the procession of the Indian, the hunter, the trader, the cattleman, the pioneer farmer, had passed by and thriving towns and cultivated countryside developed in its wake. In tracing civilization from east to west within our country we follow a transit from an organized society to one of rude beginnings, quite as obviously as in tracing the transit from Europe to America.

It is necessary first to notice, somewhat gloomily, that civilization, generally speaking, declines when it strikes the frontier. This might almost be advanced as the second law of transit. Compare the intellectual tone of New England in the sixteen-forties with that at the end of the century, and the contrast is depressing. We may quote from the unpublished autobiography of President Samuel Johnson, of King's College, writing of his student days in New England about 1714: "The condition of learning (as well as everything else) was very low in these times, indeed much lower than in the earlier time while those yet lived who had had their education in England and first settled the country. These were now gone off the stage and their sons fell greatly short of their acquirements, as through the necessity of the times they could give but little attention to the business of education." The concentrated light of local history reveals this falling off; the late Henry R. Stiles in his minute review of *Ancient Windsor,* for example, observed that the second generation did not fill the places of the fathers. The earlier leaders had been trained in Cambridge, England, the later in Cambridge, Massachusetts—and there was a difference. It is easy to forget the quiddities of the library and drawing-room when living in a forest, and even in the extreme instance to relapse into barbarism as "squaw men."

In 1840, to advance somewhat more than a century in time and less than a thousand miles in space, the percentage of illiteracy in Indiana was fourteen; ten years later it was twenty-two. Appreciation of special training fell apace. Neither the Indiana frontier, nor any other, developed any overpowering respect for the professional man; it must be remembered that it was Andrew Jackson who deprofessionalized the civil service of the country. In 1817 the Indiana legislature, made up of men who had come from older communities, laid down careful rules for examination by the courts of all candidates for the bar; in accordance with procedure slowly worked out by centuries of experience, the judges in the cases tried before them expounded the law leaving to the jury the decision of the facts. But the constitution of 1851 permitted any citizen of ordinary decency to practise law, and allowed the jury, however ignorant, to determine what rules of law should be applied. The legal standards for medical practice were likewise relaxed in the frontier environment to make way for the botanical practitioners and other short-schooled doctors. In fact, it must be confessed that medical standards in general declined for a time after their transit to America.

The delicate plant can not immediately take root in a wilderness. Men and women of refinement can not easily become frontiersmen, as the colony of Napoleonic exiles at Demopolis, in Alabama, sadly illustrates. If one such could, he would soon find that his mind was starving. The frontier can not furnish an environment of sympathy. Many Europeans later known throughout the world as great masters have in their youth comtemplated a removal to America. Robert Boyle and Comenius thought seriously of following the suggestion of their friend John Winthrop, Jr., and crossing to Connecticut, but had they set up in our half-won countryside would one have become the father of modern chemistry and the other the father of modern education? Goethe planned to come, but as an American would he have written *Faust?* Coleridge and Southey had a romantic project of starting new careers in the upper Susquehanna Valley, but had they done so in the seventeen-nineties would they rank to-day among the great figures of literature? Whatever momentum such men might have had upon arrival their mental energy would have spent itself without sympathy, constructive criticism, and the stimulus of competition. The frontier can not furnish support for its own distinguished minds; generally they must reach development in the metropolis. "It is certainly remarkable," observed the writer of an article on Lindley Murray in the *Literary Magazine* for January, 1804, "that the natives of America who have arrived at eminence in arts and letters have done so in a foreign country." Really it was not remarkable at all. Would Benjamin West have become a painter of world renown if he had stayed in Pennsylvania? Would Benjamin Thompson have discovered the laws of heat as a citizen of Woburn, Massachusetts? But we can not too closely limit Omnipotence; miracles may happen and genius flourish in an unpromising environment —there was Franklin, for example.

The frontier is handicapped by lack of leisure and by the migratoriness of its life, as well as its distance from the centres of culture. But while it forgets its heritage somewhat, its equalitarian standards, resulting from the homogeneity of its population, lead it to diffuse whatever it retains. It stands hopefully for mass education and therefore lays a broad, firm basis for culture as it may be imported and developed. Leisure as it comes is rather evenly distributed and Culture, written with a large C, becomes everybody's business. The woman's club of the modern type was born in the Middle West in the eighteen-fifties.

But this culture, as we have seen, is constantly modified, or, if you will, increased, by contacts with the outside world. There are constantly presented new modes from which the community may choose for imitation. The accidental carriers, the "Typhoid Marys" of ideas, are sometimes effective and sometimes not; probably the carrier's influence is most immediate when he is not much unlike the mass he touches. Indiana was mentioned, a few lines back, as a typical frontier society a hundred years ago, and perhaps the Hoosier State will serve as well as any other for our illustrations. Robert Owen's "boatload of knowledge" that pushed up the Wabash to New Harmony in 1826 was doubtless of considerable consequence to the little world of political theorists, but not much to Indiana. An elaborate history of the state has been written without mentioning the socialistic experiment which happened to take place upon its soil but which had small part in its development. It would be difficult, indeed impossible, to trace the course of the myriad unconscious carriers who were effective. Perhaps most culture, though seldom the highest, has been transmitted by such means. But many of the carriers are conscious, resolute, and constructive, yet fully sympathetic with the frontier; we may call them the civilizers. It has taken spendid courage to assume and carry through this rôle. In the early days it took physique. Could the circuit rider thrash the rowdies, the "scorners," who stood ready to break up the meeting? Could the school-teacher's digestion endure the ordeal of boarding around a neighborhood devoted to a hog-and-hominy cuisine? Could the conscientious doctor survive the forty-mile rides through the wintry forest?

But quite apart from these raw perils patent to the sense, the civilizer always took a risk. Could he hew a way to the light through the thicket of ignorance and prejudice, as the previous pioneer had chopped his way through oak and cypress, or would he succumb and shamefully settle down to live like others in a mental shade? Was the frontier yet ready for him? There comes to mind the case of Baynard R. Hall, the first functionary in the higher education of Indiana. Indiana wanted him, but only moderately; education was not yet its ruling passion, and it paid him but two hundred dollars for a year's instruction. It was not the money that thrilled him, however, and held him to his purpose of building a state university, but the thought that he was, as he said, "the very first man since the creation of the world to read Greek in the New Purchase." It was pleasing to his vanity, no doubt, to reflect that he was the man —young professional men have often been moved to go west by the thought that they would seem more important there than at home—but I think, as a whole, the civilizers have thought as much of civilization as of themselves. The material compensation probably did not tempt them. The circuit riders got an annual payment of from fifty dollars to two hundred, and that would have been better if it had not so often been paid in "dicker," in beef, corn, butter, potatoes, leather, buckwheat flour, feathers, coon-skins, and the like.

It took courage, too, to carry to the frontier the instruments of civilization such as the printing press. This is not the tool of a man, but of a community; and to sustain it the community must be literate, moderately well-to-do, and with an economic life sufficiently organized to need an advertising medium. There was certainly a risk in taking it to the frontier. The covered wagon is familiar to us all as an epic theme, but behind it have come other arks and vehicles and beasts of precious burden, freighted with as fine a hope and driven by as stout a courage, carrying, indeed, the instruments and records of the human mind. Across the screen of memory toils the Conestoga-wagon team over the Alleghenies, in 1786, to the shabby little river town at the forks of the Ohio, laden with the press, the type, the ink, the paper that were to make up John Scull's Pittsburgh *Gazette;* then from here a short year later there sets out the flat-boat of John Bradford with another rude printing press and some type cut out of dogwood, which, after being jolted into sad confusion on the rough wood-way from the river down to Lexington, does full part to build the fame of that "Athens of the West"; and then in 1804, when seventeen years of effort have driven the pioneer's axe deep into the old Northwest, Elihu Stout, a printer on this paper, supported by the same faith, straps a press and type athwart pack-horses and threads the path to far-away Vincennes. The advance of civilization by *Gazettes!*

In the pageant of the arts and sciences these humble equipages have their place, and the men who guided them. It was a desperate enterprise. Take, for example, the first newspaper in the capital of Indiana, the Indianapolis *Gazette,* printed on a clumsy Ramage press in 1882, a year after the city's foundation, in a one-room log cabin, "part of which was occupied for a family residence." The nearest post-office was sixty miles away, so that President Monroe's message delivered in the first week of December was prime news in February. The picture can be reproduced a hundred times in American history. The paper-making frontier crossed the Alleghenies not long after that of the press; it was only six years behind in Kentucky and five in the Western Reserve; but it was not till 1820 that the first type foundry was established in the Mississippi Valley. Meanwhile, books were published, especially at Cincinnati. It had taken the printing business in all its essentials thirty-five years to cross the mountains, but in the colonial period it had taken a hundred and thirty-three years to cross the sea.

Herbert Spencer's famous law was that life proceeds from homogeneity to heterogeneity, from the simple to the complex. On the frontier one can actually watch the evolution of social species. In New England during the eighteenth century there were few clergymen, doctors, or lawyers but did some farming; certainly this was true in the early days of Indiana. Consider the case of the Reverend John M. Dickey, in Washington County in 1815, as it is reported: "Mr. Dickey . . . aided the support of his family by farming on a small scale, teaching a singing class, and writing deeds, wills, and advertisements. He also surveyed land and sometimes taught school." But this clergyman-schoolmaster-lawyer was already on the way to specialization, as apparently he did not practise medicine. Seventeenth-century ministers, even important ones like Giles Firmin and Gershom Bulkeley, had cured the body with the soul, exhibiting, as Cotton Mather said, an "Angelical conjunction." It would be interesting for a state historical survey to trace graphically on the map the moving frontier of the professional family doctor in its state, to see how far he was behind the thin edge of the population mass; then to see the line of first throw-off from that stem, the trained apothecary; then the line of the second branch, the dentist; then that of the third, the modern surgeon; then those of successive specialties. History is an enterprise in space as well as in time, and such maps we now recognize as an important part of its records. No one can tell what deductions might be made if such a series were set before a scholar; for the map reveals as well as illustrates. It must be remembered that it was in examining the census maps of 1890 that Professor Frederick J. Turner saw in many phases the significance of the frontier in American history.

We speak as if this march of civilization were the stuff of history alone, yet a journey from one ocean to the other would reveal how it proceeds to-day. Where is the public library frontier in 1927? The picture gallery frontier? The chamber-music frontier? What is passing into New Mexico? Montana? Arkansas? Quite obviously it is not wholly a matter of East and West. In each region throughout the country there is a centre which as a provincial town, relatively speaking, receives its culture, and as a metropolis transmits it in every direction to its countryside. Each province profoundly modifies the culture it receives; each metropolis is affected by its provinces, which throw back challenges as well as contributions in the shape of their ambitious youth, who in their energy and more equalitarian standards tend to break up old stratifications —but all this is another story. It is enough here to remember that civilization is still in transit; as we move about we are all carriers in greater or less degree, and each can say with Tennyson's Ulysses, "I am a part of all that I have met."

LOUIS B. WRIGHT (b. 1899) was for many years a member of the Huntington Library research staff. Since 1948 he has served as Director of the Folger Shakespeare Library in Washington. Among his books are *Middle Class Culture in Elizabethan England* (1935) and *The Cultural Life of the American Colonies* (1957). In *Culture on the Moving Frontier* (1955) Professor Wright demonstrates the ways in which the traditional learning and cultural heritage moved to successive frontiers as American pioneers sought to prevent reversion to barbarism. His interest in both the renaissance culture of England and the American colonial period qualifies him in an unusual way to show how the American pioneer purposely and systematically sought to preserve the English heritage of the past.*

Louis B. Wright

The Inheritance of Fundamental English Qualities

The struggle between the good and evil angels for the soul of man was a popular theme in medieval drama. English audiences about 1425 delighted in a play called *The Castle of Perserverance* in which the Seven Virtues and the Four Daughters of God defended the fortress against the Devil and the Seven Deadly Sins who were determined to capture Mankind and make him their own. Although we have long since forgotten the old play, we are still witnesses of the perennial struggle for man's soul. Indeed, the development of American society from the first settlement at Jamestown until the latest outpost in the Far West has exemplified the contest between the powers of darkness and the forces of light for the soul and mind of the American citizen. The history of society on the ever moving frontier might well be cast in the metaphor of this morality play. As we have grown increasingly more secular, the dramatis personae have concerned themselves with the minds rather than the souls of men, but the two can never be separated. Under whatever names the contestants may be called, the conflict goes on.

The freedom, the lack of restraint, and the lawlessness of the American frontier have received such dramatic emphasis in the literature describing the movement of settlers across this continent that we are prone to forget other more significant characteristics. We are likely to overlook the unspectacular efforts of godly and law-abiding folk to establish old patterns

*From Louis B. Wright, *Culture on the Moving Frontier* (Bloomington, Ind., Indiana University Press, 1955), pp. 11-16, 20-21, 28-32, 39, 43-45, 238-241.

of behavior. Yet on every frontier, as the American continent was settled, a group who sometimes described themselves self-consciously as the "better element" waged a persistent warfare against the disintegrating forces which the liberty of a wild country unloosed. This group were the conservators of traditional conduct, traditional ways of doing things, traditional manners and morals, and they sought to preserve and perpetuate the ancient inheritance of things of the mind and spirit. In short, they tried to reproduce in the new environment the best of the civilized way of life they had previously known. Sometimes this better element was a minority, but a potent minority who, if they lost an occasional battle, usually managed in some fashion to win the war against the powers of darkness. The conservation and perpetuation of traditional civilization in each newly settled region of the country have not received dramatic acclaim; they are not the subjects for stirring novels or sensational movies; but few characteristics have had a greater importance in the development of American society as we know it today. The ideas and traditions that determined the quality of American character were, of course, British, for the dominant stock in the colonial period was British. Other nations and races contributed their quotas to the early settlements, but at most their influence merely modified prevailing British characteristics. Although French Huguenots, German Pietists, Dutch Calvinists, and other non-British groups played a prominent part in the development of certain regions, their cultures flourished only in relatively small areas and in time were enveloped or overlaid with elements of British civilization.

British culture has demonstrated a remarkable vitality, and an even more remarkable capacity for the assimilation and transformation of other cultures into the British pattern. For example, despite the large proportion of Dutch in New York, that colony, by the end of the seventeenth century, had already absorbed so much from its English conquerors that it could not be thought of as an alien land. It had become an English colony, and Dutchmen in New York City had begun to ape English fashions. If certain characteristics of Dutch architecture, of Dutch cooking, and of Dutch folklore became a part of the permanent inheritance of New York, nevertheless the prevailing influences were British. The Dutch inheritance served merely to give a special flavor to British culture which took root and flourished in New York. So it was in all of the thirteen colonies, and in the later colonies which they in turn sent out to people the rest of the American continent. Many races and nationalities contributed to the stream of settlers who went West, and many influences modified the mode of life which they adopted, but the vigor of British culture was such that it gave to all the cities and towns along the route of the westward migration a characteristic stamp. Different as are Philadelphia, New York, Boston, Cincinnati, Lexington, Indianapolis, St. Louis, San Francisco, and Seattle, they all have a cultural common denominator that goes back to the seventeenth century and the stock of ideas that British settlers brought with them.

These ideas were a part of an ancient inheritance which had been greatly enriched in the sixteenth century when Englishmen responded to a new spirit alive in the world. They had wakened to a fresh realization of the interest and importance of the world across the Channel. They had also become aware of the value of Spanish gold from the New World, and they took what they considered a proper share of this wealth. But English acquisitiveness was not confined to the material riches of gold and silver. They pillaged the intellectual closets of Europe and brought home ideas and information which stimulated all England and brought about a Golden Age of literature and learning. Stirred to the depths of its soul by the religious revolution taking place in Europe, England underwent a transformation in its spiritual life. The controversies and ideological conflicts that the Reformation unleashed affected every phase of English life for two centuries, and in time influenced the quality of American civilization. For these and many other reasons, students of American history should begin their studies, not with the settlement of Jamestown, or even with Raleigh's abortive attempts at colonization, but with the intellectual and spiritual upheavals in Europe that began in the late fifteenth century and gathered force during the next century and a half. Most of the ideas that our colonial ancestors brought with them received their modern shape in this period.

Modern America is so polyglot, and social historians have devoted so much attention in recent years to analyzing and describing the multifarious European, Asiatic, and African influences in the development of American life that we are now in danger of underestimating and even of forgetting the oldest, the most persistent, and the most vigorous strain in our cultural inheritance. Great Britain's influence is still so strong that it subtly determines qualities of mind and character in Americans who cannot claim a drop of Anglo-Saxon blood. This is not to say that these influences necessarily make Americans pro-English. Colonel McCormick and his Anglophobe confreres in the *Chicago Tribune's* empire need have no worries about the un-American nature of this foreign element. Indeed, they are just as much under its spell as any others, even if they do not know it or would not admit it. If there were no other legacy from the past except the English language and its literature, that alone would be sufficient to explain the durability and strength of the tradition.

The long struggle to transplant a civilized way of life to the wilderness began with the arrival of the first Englishmen at Jamestown in 1607, and the nature of that struggle was characteristic of that which went on in many later wilderness communities. The early settlers were an unruly lot, more intent upon finding gold or some other quick source of wealth than upon establishing a stable society. Yet they were not so far gone in greed and sin that they forgot to bring along a parson, one Robert Hunt; and perhaps the first permanent structure erected at Jamestown was a church.

These men, living in a pestilential marsh within earshot and bowshot of the Indians, were not allowed to lapse into savagery. When Captain John Smith sent a detail of gentlemen to chop wood, they blistered their hands and swore at the pain, an offense against decorum which caused their commander to decree a proper punishment—a can of cold water poured down the offender's sleeve for each oath. The picture of Captain Smith or his deputy counting oaths and meting out punishment has in it the elements of comic opera, but it signifies a determination to whip the lawless pioneers into an ordered and decent community. . . .

Faced with the hard life exacted by an agricultural economy, weak or indolent folk might have lapsed into barbarism. But the men and women who established themselves in this country were neither weak nor lazy, and they had an almost grim determination to reproduce modes of life which they had respected and honored in the old country. Civilization did not come to the river lands of Virginia and Maryland as a spontaneous growth. It was cultivated with even greater effort than the planters gave to the growing of tobacco and livestock. Men and women worked hard to retain their own intellectual and spiritual inheritance and to pass on to their children the accomplishments and qualities of character which they most admired.

The development of the Tidewater aristocracy in the Chesapeake Bay area is proof of the vitality of the concepts of the country families in England, the country gentry. Pretentious as are the genealogies of many Virginia families, actually their origins are extremely vague. Though many of them think they are descended from some noble or royal ancestor —King Edward III is frequently claimed —most of them have no clear proof of their ancestry on the other side of the Atlantic. Their first American ancestors were immigrants hoping to improve their economic lot, like immigrants in any age; they would not have left England had they been important or prosperous. Marcus Jernegan, weary with listening to fabulous genealogies, once remarked that if Virginians would quit looking for their ancestors in Burke's peerage and start searching the calendars of Newgate Prison they would come nearer finding them. But who the Virginians were before they came to this country is less important than what they became once they were here. Those with enough capital or influence to acquire substantial holdings of land quickly set about establishing themselves as country gentlemen as nearly like the county families of England as they could make themselves. . . .

Those who failed to meet the challenge also produced a society of their own to which American folklore is much beholden. William Byrd encountered some of them in the backwoods of North Carolina when he was surveying the dividing line. Fertile soil and a benign climate made life so easy that these North Carolinians succumbed to a slothful existence little better than that of the Indians. The men were accustomed to lie snoring in bed through the early hours of the day, Byrd writes. "Then, after Stretching and Yawning for half an Hour, they light their Pipes, and under the Protection of a cloud of Smoak, venture out into the open Air; tho', if it happens to be never so little cold, they quickly return Shivering into the Chimney corner. When the weather is mild, they stand leaning with both their arms upon the corn-field fence, and gravely consider whether they had best go and take a Small Heat at the Hough: but generally find reasons to put it off till another time. Thus they loiter away their Lives, like Solomon's Sluggard."

And Professor Toynbee, describing some of the descendants of these colonial sluggards, finds that "the Appalachian 'mountain people' today are no better than barbarians. They have relapsed into illiteracy and witchcraft. They suffer from poverty, squalor and ill-health. They are the American counterparts of the latter-day white barbarians of the Old World —Riffs, Albanians, Kurds, Pathans, and Hairy Ainus; but whereas these latter are belated survivals of an ancient barbarism, the Appalachians present the melancholy spectacle of a people who have acquired civilization and then lost it." Describing the barbarizing influence of the American frontier, Toynbee quotes the most famous of the historians of the frontier, Frederick Jackson Turner, in support of his ideas about the "spiritual malady of barbarization" in frontier societies.

But both Turner and Toynbee discount or overlook the potent minority of culture bearers who plant and cultivate the elements of traditional civilization on each successive frontier. That was the significance of the planters of the Chesapeake Bay region. These men exerted such a powerful influence and established such a vital civilization, albeit a rural society, that their ideas and concepts dominated a great region for the generations which followed them. The English tradition was so thoroughly established that the South has remained the section of the United States most sympathetic to Britain and things British.

While the Chesapeake Bay agrarians were establishing a picket line of English civilization along their waterways, New Englanders were organizing towns and reproducing the kind of traditional culture which their religion and their mores dictated. Because geographical conditions favored trade and commerce instead of an exclusively agrarian economy, New England became a region of villages and towns instead of a commonwealth of scattered plantations. The mere physical fact of grouping in close communities made the struggle against barbarism much simpler in New England than in the South. Furthermore, many of the New England settlers came as closely knit groups with definite ideas of the kind of society which they proposed to establish. They were simply transferring to what they hoped would be a more favorable environment a religious and social culture which they were determined to defend with all of the resources at their command.

Puritanism, which in some variety predominated throughout New England, was a militant faith, full of vigor and strength. The force and energy of the Puritans' determination to civilize whatever land they occupied affected the whole later course of American history. Whether the Puritans were operating in Boston in 1635 or in San Francisco in 1849, they made their influence felt. The godless trembled and the ignorant soon found themselves being instructed. No Puritan was ever willing to tolerate either devil or dunce.

Although seventeenth-century Puritans had no monopoly of piety and moral rectitude, they practiced more intensely than others certain austere and prudential virtues which coincided with the ideals of the rising middle class. We do not have to agree entirely with Max Weber's famous thesis on capitalism and the Protestant ethic to concede that the Puritan code of behavior was highly effective in developing the doctrine of success which has become a part of the American social dogma. The Puritans were not the only ones who taught the virtues of diligence, thrift, and sobriety, but they emphasized these qualities to such a degree that extravagance became a cardinal sin and work was regarded as a worthy end in itself. Having forsworn waste of either time or money, and having made a virtue of unceasing diligence in his calling, a Puritan, unless he had phenomenally bad luck, could hardly escape material success. Furthermore, he devised an educational system intended to sharpen his wits and make his mind a more effective instrument for dealing with his fellow men. It is small wonder that the Yankee in the nineteenth century became a byword for resourcefulness and shrewdness. Actually he represented the ultimate flowering of the seventeenth-century middle class who were strongly Puritan in their backgrounds.

The political doctrine of Manifest Destiny which played such an important part in westward expansion was a natural outgrowth of the Puritan belief that they were God's chosen people. New Englanders, whether in the seventeenth century or in later periods, have always had a strong conviction of their divine calling to "improve" the world. From the beginning in this country they have been inspired apostles of their particular civilization, and wherever they have gone, from Massachusetts to Ohio and thence to the Pacific Coast, they have displayed a zeal for religion, learning, and social improvement in accordance with their traditional ideas. If we cannot credit Puritan New Englanders with the entire responsibility for civilizing the West, we can discern evidence of their intense activity in nearly every locality. They were a busy and convinced social group, intent upon reproducing their society wherever they went. In most places they succeeded, sometimes too well. . . .

Other religious sects paralleled the New England Puritans in their zeal to maintain the elements of traditional civilization in the backwoods. Indeed, the most notable contribution in the second half of the colonial period was made by Scotch-Irish Presbyterians, chiefly Scots from Northern Ireland. After the turn of the eighteenth century, they poured into America, principally through the port of Philadelphia, though some entered at Charleston, South Carolina, and at other ports. Pushing past the older settlements, they made their way to the back country and fanned out down the river valleys of Pennsylvania and moved on into adjacent territory. They became the typical frontiersmen of the period, the spearheads of white penetration of Indian territory. . . .

Struggle as colonial Americans might to retain the cultivation of the mother country, they sometimes found themselves fighting a losing battle. The hardships of the wilderness were too great to leave much time for anything except the bitter struggle for survival. The second generation of Americans, even in such literate spots as Boston, appeared to be less cultivated that their elders, but perhaps, as Professor Samuel Eliot Morison has suggested, they merely reflected a prosaic period. A significant fact is that colonial Americans themselves were so conscious of their loss from the dimming of the cultural lamps that they were eternally trying to improve the sources of illumination.

The desire for self-improvement has been one of the most characteristic qualities in Americans from the earliest times to the present day. One has only to read the advertisements of correspondence courses and manuals for self-help in our periodicals to realize how widespread is that appeal today. Benjamin Franklin's *Autobiography* gives a vivid account of the procedure by which one of the greatest colonials educated himself and made himself proficient in the useful knowledge of the past. Franklin is an excellent example of the transmission of ideas from the Old World to the New, for much of his pragmatic philosophy which has so profoundly influenced American thinking had its origin in the ideas of the English middle class of the late sixteenth and early seventeenth centuries.

One of the works that influenced Franklin was *The Spectator* which he read and deliberately imitated. Franklin was not the only American who found the works of Joseph Addison and Richard Steele both entertaining and improving. Few English authors had greater influence upon eighteenth-century Americans than these two, and the reason is not hard to find. Addison and Steele provided sound and "improving" reading matter designed to teach good manners, decorum, decency, and urbanity with the least possible pain to the reader. Their ideas coincided with the common-sense, middle-class notions which dominated most American thinking, whether of the agrarian aristocracy or the trading classes in such centers as Boston and Philadelphia. Implicit in *The Spectator* was the ideal of self-improvement which appealed especially to colonial Americans and became a part of our social dogma.

The Spectator was, of course, only one of many influences which helped to shape second and third generation Americans into the mold of civilized Englishmen. The conscious effort to reproduce English society succeeded almost too well in certain areas. Charleston, South Carolina, for example, did its best to be a replica of London in little and imitated the good as well as the bad qualities of the British capital. Many Charlestonians went to London for business and professional reasons and brought back manners, habits, and customs of the metropolis. Many others imported the current books and periodicals which gave them an insight into the civilized world across the Atlantic.

In all the urban centers in colonial America the same thing was happening. For all of its polyglot population, Philadelphia, the largest of the American towns at the end of the colonial period —and the second city in the British empire—became a center of British culture. That is not to say that German and French influences were invisible, or that Quaker Philadelphians were like Anglican Charlestonians, but that the most important influences at work in that society were English, and London was the focal point from which Philadelphians imported ideas. From the towns and cities along the seaboard, the elements of civilization percolated to the most distant frontiers. Long before the end of the colonial period, British culture was already penetrating the rudest settlements to the west. . . .

An infinite variety of agencies, from parsons in their pulpits to shirt-sleeved editors of ragged little weekly papers, labored to bring law and order, decency, learning, and cultivation to a succession of frontier regions beginning with the Atlantic littoral in the seventeenth century and ending with the Pacific Coast and the interior Great Basin in the nineteenth. The task of molding an inchoate mass of people from many nations and races into something approaching a homogeneous society was not easy, but miraculously it succeeded.

We used to be fond of talking about the melting pot of America. But what did the component elements melt into? Into something called an American, and that American had a prototype across the seas who was responsible for the American's language, his basic laws, his fundamental liberties, and much of his manners, customs, and social attitudes. That prototype was British, and primarily English. The English tradition was the strongest element of civilization on the successive frontiers. It had an incredible power of assimilation and transmutation. At the end of the eighteenth century a Frenchman naturalized in New York, Hector St. John De Crèvecoeur, wrote a famous essay asking the question, "What Is an American?" And he answered by declaring that "the American is a new man" assimilated from a "mixture of English, Scotch, Irish, French, Dutch, German, and Swedes. From this promiscuous breed that race now called Americans have arisen." Two significant factors were responsible for the assimilation of these people into the new American: the economic opportunities of the young country and the cultural traditions of the predominant English. Whatever the national and racial origins of American immigrants might be, within two generations, most Americans so reflected English ideas and attitudes that many of them might have passed for Englishmen.

In a book full of salty wisdom entitled *Our English Heritage,* Gerald W. Johnson recognized the assimilative quality of the English tradition and pointed out the nature of our inheritance. "The England that still holds a powerful grip upon the thoughts and acts of the American people, including those of non-English origin," writes Mr. Johnson, "is not the realm of the English king, nor the institutions created by the English people. It is nothing so tangible, nothing definable in materialistic terms. It is a story, partly history, partly legend, largely poetry and drama." It is the story of the plain man's struggle and rise from serfdom to the greatest liberty under law that any man has ever known. It is also an inheritance of practicality from a nation of shop-keepers who taught us that commerce is honorable and that fair play in business is part of the code of decent men. Locke, Hobbes, and Herbert Spencer all contributed their theories to English philosophy which has influenced us, but Mr. Johnson observes quite correctly that most of us know nothing of them directly. "The English philosophy that still sways the thoughts and acts of millions [of Americans] who never saw inside of a college is none of these," Mr. Johnson adds. "It is English faith in gradualism linked with compromise, English faith in ability as at least equal to heredity, and English faith in commerce as a better instrument of conquest than war." The pragmatism which permeates American thought is essentially an inheritance from middle-class England.

A quality in us that our British brethren today find hard to bear is the conviction, with its corollaries, that we are God's chosen people. We are loud is the assertion that this is God's country; that our standard of living is the greatest blessing of mankind, and that universal bliss will come when the rest of the world has as many refrigerators, washing machines, and television sets as we possess; that the American constitution is the world's finest instrument of government; and that we are called upon to export our kind of civilization to all mankind. But this quality too is an inheritance from the British. Manifest Destiny was not an invention of President Polk and his generation or of any American, for that matter. Seventeenth-century English Puritans were convinced that they were God's saints destined to inherit this world and the next. Successive generations of the British were certain that God spoke English, and they heard a clear call to go out to the ends of the earth, to sell their goods, to bear the white man's burden, to rule the inefficient, and to spread their civilization. Americans expanding westward in the nineteenth century merely fell into a normal practice and devised a slogan to justify their actions.

For better or for worse, we have inherited the fundamental qualities in our culture from the British. For that reason we need to take a long perspective of our history, a perspective which views America from at least the period of the first Tudor monarchs and lets us see the gradual development of our common civilization, its transmission across the Atlantic, and its expansion and modification as it was adapted to conditions in the Western Hemisphere. We should not overlook other influences which have affected American life, influences from France, Holland, Spain, Germany, Scandinavia, and the rest of Europe, and also influences from Asia and Africa. But we must always remember that such was the vigor of British culture that it assimilated all others. That is not to say that we have been transmogrified into Englishmen, or that we are even Anglophile in sentiment. But we cannot escape an inheritance which has given us some of our sturdiest and most lasting qualities.

OSCAR HANDLIN (b. 1915), Professor of History at Harvard University since 1954, established his reputation through his studies of American immigration patterns. *The Uprooted,* from which this selection is taken, is a highly poetic and evocative saga of the immigrant's voyage to the United States and the problems he experienced here. In this selection Handlin is concerned with the psychological effects of of the process of immigration on the world view of the immigrating peasant. He finds the process essentially conservative, reinforcing, in the face of change, the traditional modes of life and thought.*

Oscar Handlin

Immigration and the Reinforcement of the Traditional

Often, they would try to understand. They would think about it in the pauses of their work, speculate sometimes as their minds wandered, tired, at the close of a long day.

What had cut short the continuous past, severed it from the unrelated present? Immigration had transformed the entire economic world within which the peasants had formerly lived. From surface forms to inmost functionings, the change was complete. A new setting, new activities, and new meanings forced the newcomers into radically new roles as producers and consumers of goods. In the process, they became, in their own eyes, less worthy as men. They felt a sense of degradation that raised a most insistent question: Why had this happened?

More troubling, the change was not confined to economic matters. The whole American universe was different. Strangers, the immigrants could not locate themselves; they had lost the polestar that gave them their bearings. They would not regain an awareness of direction until they could visualize themselves in their new context, see a picture of the world as it appeared from this perspective. At home, in the wide frame of the village, their eyes had taken in the whole of life, had brought to their perceptions a clearly defined view of the universe. Here the frame narrowed down, seemed to reveal only

*From *The Uprooted* by Oscar Handlin, by permission of Atlantic, Little, Brown and Co., pp. 94–99, 102–116. Copyright 1951, by Oscar Handlin.

fragmentary distorted glimpses that were hardly reminiscent of the old outlines.

The peasants brought with them from their life on the soil the preconceptions and basic assumptions that had controlled their attitudes and influenced their actions. Before emigration they had lived in intimate contact with nature, never much removed from the presence of the objects of the physical universe. All around were things not made by men's hands, things that coexisted with men. Between these things and men there were differences. But they were also held together by the most powerful ligatures, for the universe was not made up of entirely disparate, disconnected objects but of elements which varied only imperceptibly from each other. Men and things were alike subject to natural processes, alike responsive to the same moving forces.

Everything the peasant saw about him was, like himself, a being. All the objects of nature, of whatever shape or form or substance, were literally animated, perhaps to greater or lesser degrees, but all were essentially capable of life and growth. All were God's creatures, man and the beasts too, and also the trees, the meadows, the stars, the sun, fire and water, the days of the week and the seasons of the year. Yes, even clods and stones had being.

In all these entities, the characteristics of animation were the same as those among men. All had individuality. So, the animals of the barnyard had each his own name, and those of field and forest —not so intimately known—were represented by imaginary titled heads of their species. Trees, rocks, springs, had also each its appellation, and every day of the year its own designation from the saint or festival that gave it its quality.

With the name went the ascription of personality: each being had character, had the capacity for action, had some degree of volition. All the objects of nature, being animate, had understanding enough to react meaningfully to conditions about them. They had a kind of intelligence which, while different from man's, was not necessarily inferior. In fact, other beings knew things humans did not know: birds and beasts could foretell changes in the weather; at the approach of danger, geese would fall a-clamoring in the enclosures, dogs run nervously about. Animals even had a sense to judge bad action; for instance, bees, it was said, would not stay with a thief.

It was incumbent upon men, dealing with these beings, to be careful, to stay on good terms with them, to give them their due lest they retaliate. Each day thus had its own character and, if not respected, would return after a year to exact vengeance. A violated tree, or one not properly bound with straw, would bear no fruit; neglected land would yield no grain; the mistreated cow would give no milk; an unclean fire would go out. Accidental injuries to these beings, when they occurred, had to be explained and the victims appeased if possible. The utmost caution was worth while, for those who won them over could use the foresight of animals to good advantage. So, the friendly birds, if only rightly understood, could with certainty give the sign for the best time for sowing.

Among all natural beings there existed also the relationship of solidarity. All were so connected with each other that what happened to any one affected every other. If the birds flew away to the woods, then the snow would soon decide to fall. If the sparrows were permitted to eat cherries in the summer that would help the grain to thrive. Such attributes as richness and the capacity for growth were therefore transferable and fecundity could be bestowed by one object on another. The peasant rubbed fertile soil onto his cow to be sure she would bear often.

There were also special kinds of solidarity within species of things. All animals were particularly related and, when danger threatened, warned each other, at times indeed could speak among themselves. There was a more intimate relationship within each class of animals; the cows lowing softly to one another had their own secrets. This was the identical solidarity that men felt for other men. Did not the peasants' lives revolve about their membership in a natural community that cared for them?

To whatever degree it was general, solidarity among all beings sprang from the common situation in which they found themselves. All the objects of nature were engaged in growth. They participated thereby in the same struggle against decay. The solidarity among them was the inner recognition that man and beast, plant and living soil, in some measure fought the same battle. A breach of solidarity was treachery in the face of the enemy of all and merited the severest punishment. To cut down a fruit tree, to kill a stork, to waste, was a hideous disruption of the order of nature, an invitation to calamitous retaliation.

A sacrifice was justified only when it involved a lesser retreat before decay in the interests of greater growth. Thus it was proper to clear trees in order to bring new lands under cultivation; increased production would expiate the destruction. So, also, animals gave up their lives, willingly as it were, to the end that men might eat. But even in such legitimate instances, it was best to be cautious, to act according to appropriate forms. Special rites to ward off unfavorable consequences accompanied the slaughter or any other measure that might involve some hidden breach of solidarity.

If man had to proceed warily in encounters with the world of natural objects, he was compelled to be doubly careful when it came to the mysterious realm of unnatural beings that also existed about him. This realm was not continuous with his own world. It was a dread level of being, inhabited by spirits of many kinds that took many shapes. Fairies, elves, leprechauns might perhaps be visualized, though not reliably; but no mind could conceive of the variety of forms that might be assumed by vampires, specters, souls adrift on earth or released for some special end from hell or purgatory. These beings could enter the natural world, but there was no solidarity between them and the objects of nature.

The affairs of the spirits were ever a source of concern to the peasant. They had powers beyond those of the poor human and could interfere when they liked with his own affairs—sometimes beneficently assisting him, sometimes through malice or mischief bringing utter ruin down upon the unfortunate victim who had offended them. Their imminent presence called for constant caution. They might do no more than make trouble with their pranks; or they might possess the bodies of people and animals; or they might betray men into disastrous temptations. They added an awesome dimension to a universe already terrifyingly vast. Among so many hazardous forces, the peasant had to walk carefully, be constantly alert to the presence of all the elements about him.

The safest way was to know the hidden causal connections among objects and events. Such knowledge gave some persons a measure of control over the activities of the beings about them. Command of magic—that is, of the certain ways, of the certain words, of the certain rites—would appease or neutralize hostile forces, enlist the support of friendly ones. That would give the peasant security.

Only, where was that knowledge found? The wily ones who had it would not share for nothing. In the stress of great need there was no choice but to seek out the witch or wizard who could converse with their familiar spirits. Yet everyone knew what frightful bargains were exacted for such assistance.

It was much safer, when each decision could have incalculable consequences, to follow the traditional time-proven patterns. One could seek guidance from the special vision of pilgrims, seers, and idiots. But the most certain advice came from the wise old ones who knew from the experience of the past what ways were the most reliable. Safety lay in adherence to routines that had been effective before; new actions were doomed to dangerous failure. When all was said and done, all things had their given course, and would follow that course. . . .

What is the religion of the men who live through winter and spring? It is the affirmation that life is victorious over death. Though the trees stand bare in winter, yet will they be clothed in spring with green leaves and sweet-scented blossoms. Though a man's life be sown with labor, with hardship, with blood, a crop will come of it, a harvest be reaped.

That affirmation was the peasant's faith, his own explanation of his place in the universe. But overlaid on this natural religion was one taught by the priests, a religion that stemmed from outside the village, from the monasteries, the towns, the nobility. By now Christianity was well-established, in some regions for more than a thousand years. Yet it had by no means destroyed the older order of beliefs. The magical practices and the ideas they embodied held on even in places where the Church made an effort to fight them. And more often than not, the priest was himself rooted in the village and was content to allow the peasants to identify their own notions with elements of Christian doctrine, to effect a practical if not a dogmatic reconciliation.

Christianity did add to the earlier peasant ideas a conception of sin and the faith in a supernatural redemption. The distinction between good and evil he heard reiterated from the pulpit the peasant identified with his own distinction between helpful and harmful forces. In the galaxy of spirits, the peasant found a place for the devil and his imps, operating for their own hellish purposes. To resist their designs he learned to call upon an army of saints, each with its own province and potency. In these terms, he came to think of the world as the field of battle between two spiritual communities, the divine and the demoniacal, which struggled for the soul of man.

The burden of choice, already heavy, thus became heavier. Any act now might be wrong not only in the sense that it could bring on hostile consequences, but also in the sense that it might partake of evil. A bad decision was induced by spirits who were unfriendly and also devilish, was damaging and also sinful. Man bore the weight not simply of his mistakes but of his guilt also. His lot was to suffer and, as well, to expiate.

Yet to him, in his troubled state, Christianity brought also the miracle of redemption. Poor thing that he was, his soul was yet a matter of consequence. For him the whole drama of salvation had been enacted: God had come to earth, had suffered as a man to make for all men a place in a life everlasting. Through that sacrifice had been created a community of all those who had faith, a kind of solidarity that would redress all grievances and right all wrongs, if not now, then in the far more important aftermath to life.

Therefore it is well to look not to the present but to the eternal future, not to this world in which there is nothing but trouble and woe but to the next in which will come ease and consolation. Here evil increases and multiplies like the thistles in the woods. Here all things are vain and to no purpose like the bubbles which the wind tosses up on the surface of the waters. Yet let our souls but fly to Jesus as the birds fly south in winter and they will find comfort and joy and an end to all sorrow.

And in those moments of meditation when the comfort comes, we know this hope is not merely a delusion personal to us. The evidence is in the visible community which together participates in the mystery of salvation. Within the divine universe is this village, and within this village we men. This is our reassurance; thus we know where we are in the world.

These were the contents with which the hearts and minds of the peasants were laden as they came to the New World. This was the stock of ideas on which they drew when they came to account for their situation in America, once they had arrived and were at work and the work they did seemed not fit work for a man. Now there would be new questions. Would the old answers do when these people tried to explain what had happened to them?

They found it difficult, of course, to reconstruct a coherent record out of the excess of their experience since they had left the village. Many impressions remained fragmentary, unrelated to any whole adjustment.

This they knew, though, and could not mistake it: they were lonely. In the midst of teeming cities, in the crowded tenements and the factories full of bustling men, they were lonely.

Their loneliness had more than one dimension. It had the breadth of unfamiliarity. Strange people walked about them; strange sounds assailed their inattentive ears. Hard pavements cut them off from nature in all its accustomed manifestations. Look how far they could, at the end of no street was a familiar horizon. Hemmed in by the tall buildings, they were fenced off from the realm of growing things. They had lost the world they knew of beasts and birds, of blades of grass, of sprays of idle flowers. They had acquired instead surroundings of a most outlandish aspect. That unfamiliarity was one aspect of their loneliness.

Loneliness had also the painful depth of isolation. The man who once had been surrounded with individual beings was here cast adrift in a life empty of all but impersonal things. In the Old Country, this house in this village, these fields by these trees, had had a character and identity of their own. They had testified to the peasant's *I*, had fixed his place in the visible universe. The church, the shrine, the graveyard and the generations that inhabited it had also had their personality, had also testified to the peasant's *I*, and had fixed his place in a larger invisible universe.

In the new country, all these were gone; that was hard enough. Harder still was the fact that nothing replaced them. In America, the peasant was a transient without meaningful connections in time and space. He lived now with inanimate objects, cut off from his surroundings. His dwelling and his place of work had no relationship to him as a man. The scores of established routines that went with a life of the soil had disappeared and with them the sense of being one of a company. Therefore the peasant felt isolated and isolation added to his loneliness.

Strangeness and isolation oppressed even those who returned to the soil. They too were lonely. Everywhere, great wastes of empty land dissevered the single farm from the rest of the world. Wrapped up in the unfamiliar landscapes of prairie distance or forest solitude, the peasants found nowhere an equivalent of the village, nowhere the basis for re-establishing the solidarity of the old communal life. Therefore they were each alone, in city and in country, for that of which they had been a part was no longer about them. . . .

Every element of the immigrants' experience since the day they had left home added to this awareness of their utter helplessness. All the incidents of the journey were bound up with chance. What was the road to follow, what the ship to board, what port to make? These were serious questions. But who knew which were the right answers? Whether they survived the hazards of the voyage, and in what condition, these too were decisions beyond the control of the men who participated in it. The capricious world of the crossing pointed its own conclusion as to the role of chance in the larger universe into which the immigrants plunged.

It was the same with their lives after landing. To find a job or not, to hold it or to be fired, in these matters laborers' wills were of slight importance. Inscrutable, distant persons determined matters on the basis of remote, unknown conditions. The most fortunate immigrants, the farmers, knew well what little power they had to influence the state of the climate, the yield of the earth, or the fluctuations of the market, all the elements that determined their lot. Success or failure, incomprehensible in terms of peasant values, seemed altogether fortuitous. Time and again, the analogy occurred to them: man was helpless like the driven cog in a great machine.

Loneliness, separation from the community of the village, and despair at the insignificance of their own human abilities, these were the elements that, in America, colored the peasants' view of their world. From the depths of a dark pessimism, they looked up at a frustrating universe ruled by haphazard, capricious forces. Without the capacity to control or influence these forces men could but rarely gratify their hopes or wills. Their most passionate desires were doomed to failure; their lives were those of the feeble little birds which hawks attack, which lose strength from want of food, and which, at last surrendering to the savage blasts of the careless elements, flutter unnoticed to the waiting earth.

Sadness was the tone of life, and death and disaster no strangers. Outsiders would not understand the familiarity with death who had not daily met it in the close quarters of the steerage; nor would they comprehend the riotous Paddy funerals who had no insight of the release death brought. The end of life was an end to hopeless striving, to ceaseless pain, and to the endless succession of disappointments. There was a leaden grief for the ones who went, yet the tomb was only the final parting in a long series of separations that had started back at the village crossroads.

In this world man can only be resigned.

Illness takes a child away; from the shaft they bring a father's crippled body; sudden fire eats up a block of flimsy shanties, leaves half of each family living. There is no energy for prolonged mourning. Things are as they are and must remain so. Resist not but submit to fortune and seek safety by holding on.

In this world the notion of improvement is delusive. The best hope is that matters grow not worse. Therefore it is desirable to stand against change, to keep things as they are; the risks involved in change are incomparably more formidable than those involved in stability. There is not now less poverty, less misery, less torture, less pain than formerly. Indeed, today's evils, by their nearness, are far more oppressive than yesterday's which, after all, were somehow survived. Yesterday, by its distance, acquires a happy glow. The peasants look back (they remember they lived through yesterday; who knows if they will live through today?) and their fancy rejoices in the better days that have passed, when they were on the land and the land was fertile, and they were young and strong, and virtues were fresh. And it was better yet in their fathers' days, who were wiser and stronger than they. And it was best of all in the golden past of their distant progenitors who were every one a king and did great deeds. Alas, those days are gone, that they believed existed, and now there is only the bitter present.

In this world then, as in the Old Country, the safest way was to look back to tradition as a guide. Lacking confidence in the individual's capacity for independent inquiry, the peasants preferred to rely upon the tested knowledge of the past. It was difficult of course to apply village experience to life in America, to stretch the ancient aphorisms so they would fit new conditions. Yet that strain led not to a rejection of tradition but rather to an eager quest for a reliable interpreter. Significantly, the peasants sought to acknowledge an authority that would make that interpretation for them.

Their view of the American world led these immigrants to conservatism, and to the acceptance of tradition and authority. Those traits in turn shaped the immigrants' view of society, encouraged them to retain the peasants' regard for status and the divisions of rank. In these matters too striving was futile; it was wiser to keep each to his own station in the social order, to respect the rights of others and to exact the obligations due. For most of these people that course involved the acceptance of an inferior position. But was that not altogether realistic? The wind always blew in the face of the poor; and it was in the nature of society that some should have an abundance of possessions and others only the air they breathed.

The whole configuration of the peasant's ideas in the United States strengthened the place in his life of the established religion he brought with him. It was not only an institutional reluctance to change that held him to his faith, but also the greater need that faith satisfied in the New World.

Emigration had broken the ties with nature. The old stories still evoked emotional responses in their hearers; and the housewives still uttered imprecations and blessings and magic words to guard against the evil eye. But it was hard to believe that the whole world of spirits and demons had abandoned their familiar homes and come also across the Atlantic. It was hard too to continue to think in terms of the natural cycle of growth, of birth, death, and regeneration, away from the setting in which it was every day illustrated in peasant life.

Instead these immigrants found their Christianity ever more meaningful. Here they discovered the significance of their suffering. It was true, what the priest said, that evil was everywhere present in the world; they had themselves experienced the evidence of it. It was true they were imperfect and full of sin, not worthy of a better lot. What they tried bore no results. What they touched turned to dust.

Still all this toil and trouble was not without purpose. What seemed on the surface like the rule of chance in the world was not really so, but part of a plan. The whole of it was not yet revealed, man could not see the end, only the start, because this was not an earthly plan. Rather it extended far beyond this immediate existence and would reach its culmination in an altogether different life that came after the release of death.

Fixing his vision on that life eternal which would follow this, the peasant perceived that caprice in mundane things was an element in an ordered design. If injustice now seemed to triumph, then it was only that retribution should come after. Did the evil flourish, then would they be punished. Were the good oppressed and humiliated, it was to make their rewards the richer. This he knew was the mystery and the reason for his being in the universe.

As he participated in that other mystery of the divine sacrifice that assured him salvation, all the scattered elements of his existence became whole. Let him but have faith enough in the God Who had gone to the cross, for him; Who had come over the water, with him; and he would be repaid for the loss of his home, for the miseries of the way, and for the harshness of his present life. Not indeed in this world, but in an everlasting future. For the lonely and the isolated, for the meek and humble, for the strangers, there was hope of a sort, and consolation.

The migration to America had destroyed the context of the peasants' natural religion. Yet the resigned passivity with which they once had faced the endless round of births, deaths, and regenerations had lived on into the New World. The circumstances of their coming, alone and among foreigners, had perpetuated that sense of helplessness, had driven into the texture of their Christianity an otherworldly fatalism.

Never would they understand how this had happened or even that it had happened. They were never capable of contrasting their own situation with that of those other uprooted ones who remained in the Old World. Not all who left the village had gone to America; and the ideological development of those whose remove was to some other place in their own country took a distinctive turn of its own.

In England, for instance, the peasants displaced by the eighteenth-century revolutions in agriculture had drifted often into the growing industrial cities where they encountered circumstances as trying as those that met the transatlantic immigrants. In England too the migrants became an exploited proletariat; and their intellectual adjustment, in some respects, was analogous to that of the peasants in the United States. In England too could be seen the pessimistic reflections of a miserable life, the conservatism that grew out of resistance to inexorable changes, and the continued willingness to accept authority and to recognize status.

But there was also a significant difference. The peasants who came to America brought with them their established churches to be re-established in new communities in the New World. They transferred their faith intact and rarely were tempted to deviate from it; their foreignness alone sufficed to keep them out of the native American denominations. The peasants who migrated within England, however, did not bring their own churches with them. In London and in the rising manufacturing towns there were some churches of the established religion, of course. But they were not peasant churches; were the poor newcomers to crowd in among the pews of the well-dressed city folk, they would hardly feel at home. Those who did not remain entirely unchurched were more likely to resort to the humble chapels of the dissenters, where all benches were alike. They would be less strangers there than in the elegant edifices of the urban parishes.

A like development occurred in parts of Germany where a number of pietistic sects in the disturbed areas of the southwest weaned away some of the peasants at the end of the eighteenth century and early in the nineteenth. In Scandinavia there were similar inroads, by Methodists in Sweden, by Haugeans in Norway.

His situation made the dissenter a protester. Standing outside the established church he had to account for his difference. Incapable of justifying his affiliation by the universality of his group, he could only justify it by its particularity. This was a small group, but a select one, a group into which members were not born but into which they came. These were chosen people, people who bore a mission that demanded they be different.

Redemption for the dissenter was not the simple reward of faith; it was the product of achievement of a mission. Not resignation but a striving toward improvement was the way; and life on earth was not merely an entry into the afterlife but an opportunity by which man could demonstrate what he could make of himself. This world was therefore a place of intrinsic significance and humans had power by their wills to control their fates within it.

These people had not found their adjustment to the disruption of the old village life complicated by the transfer to a New World, a transfer so frightening that those involved in it could not venture to think outside the terms of their peasant heritage.

Sometimes the dissenting peasants, already displaced, made a second move; or more often their children did. Their American experience would then be not like that of the peasants who had come directly, but more like that of other dissenters who had never been peasants. Among the artisans and traders gathered up in the general stream of migration were several groups that had never been members of an established church, never shared fully the village views.

In that sense, the extreme of dissent, because they were altogether outside the Christian community, were the Jews. Although they had lived in close contact with the peasants for hundreds of years, they had remained apart, strangers in the society. Although the contact between the village and the Jewry was always close, often intimate, the separateness of the two persisted. Among the Jews too the role of dissenter in the midst of a solidary community evoked the consciousness that they were a chosen people, that they had a unique destiny and mission, and that the world was a field in which they could profitably labor toward improvement.

The difference that already marked the dissenters off from the peasants in advance of emigration was deepened by the experience of settlement in the United States. The dissenters had always occupied an abnormal place in peasant society; they had been the outsiders who did not belong. In America they found their position the only normal one; here, there was no established church, no solidary community; everyone to some degree was an outsider. Since the dissenters had often larger resources of capital and skill than the peasants and were more fortunate in their economic adjustment, the impact of immigration was often stimulating. They could come to identify America with their New Canaan and interpret their mission in terms of an American success.

Yet even these people were immigrants and bore with the peasant the marks of their migration. No matter how fortunate their lot, they had lost an old home and had suffered the pains of fitting themselves to a new environment. There was no danger any immigrants would grow complacent about their settlement or forget their strangeness. They had only, any of them, to think of what ideas were held by Americans longer in the land to know what a cleavage there yet was between the old and new comers. Confronted with the prevalent notions of the inevitability of progress, of the essential goodness of man and his capacity to rule his own life, of the optimistic desirability of change, peasants and dissenters alike felt a chill distrust, a determination to resist, a threat to their own ideas.

That determination was expressed in their criticism of the deficiencies of life in the United States. To the immigrants America seemed unstable; it lacked the orderly elements of existence. Without security of status or the recognition of rank, no man, no family, had a proper place in the social order. Only money talked, for Americans measured all things in terms of gold and invariably preferred the superficial and immediate to the permanent and substantial.

These reactions reflected the urge to strengthen old values and to reaffirm old ideals. Precisely because migration had subjected those to attack, it was necessary aggressively to defend them, to tolerate no change because any change might have the most threatening consequences. In that sense all immigrants were conservatives, dissenters and peasants alike. All would seek to set their ideas within a fortification of religious and cultural institutions that would keep them sound against the strange New World.

"The significance of the Frontier in American History," FREDERICK JACKSON TURNER's (1861–1932) seminal essay, was written when he was launching his professional career as Assistant Professor of History at the University of Wisconsin. The study of westward expansion became a central part of his course in the Economic and Social History of the United States and his ideas came to have a profound influence on the study and interpretation of American culture. Turner believed that the perennial rebirth of American life and institutions occasioned by the repeated westward movements furnished those forces which dominated American character.*

Frederick Jackson Turner

Successive Frontiers as Catalyst

In a recent bulletin of the Superintendent of the Census for 1890 appear these significant words: "Up to and including 1880 the country had a frontier of settlement, but at present the unsettled area has been so broken into by isolated bodies of settlement that there can hardly be said to be a frontier line. In the discussion of its extent, its westward movement, etc., it can not, therefore, any longer have a place in the census reports." This brief official statement marks the closing of a great historic movement. Up to our own day American history has been in a large degree the history of the colonization of the Great West. The existence of an area of free land, its continuous recession, and the advance of American settlement westward, explain American development.

Behind institutions, behind constitutional forms and modifications, lie the vital forces that call these organs into life and shape them to meet changing conditions. The peculiarity of American institutions is the fact that they have been compelled to adapt themselves to the changes of an expanding people—to the changes involved in crossing a continent, in winning a wilderness, and in developing at each area of this progress out of the primitive economic and political conditions of the frontier into the complexity of city life. Said Calhoun in 1817, "We are great, and rapidly—I was about to say fearfully—growing!" So saying, he touched

*From *Report of the American Historical Association for 1893* (Washington, 1894), pp. 199–227. First read as a paper at the meeting of the American Historical Association in Chicago, July 12, 1893. Footnotes omitted.

the distinguishing feature of American life. All peoples show development; the germ theory of politics has been sufficiently emphasized. In the case of most nations, however, the development has occurred in a limited area; and if the nation has expanded, it has met other growing peoples whom it has conquered. But in the case of the United States we have a different phenomenon. Limiting our attention to the Atlantic coast, we have the familiar phenomenon of the evolution of institutions in a limited area, such as the rise of representative government; the differentiation of simple colonial governments into complex organs; the progress from primitive industrial society, without division of labor, up to manufacturing civilization. But we have in addition to this a recurrence of the process of evolution in each western area reached in the process of expansion. Thus American development has exhibited not merely advance along a single line, but a return to primitive conditions on a continually advancing frontier line, and a new development for that area. American social development has been continually beginning over again on the frontier. This perennial rebirth, this fluidity of American life, this expansion westward with its new opportunities, its continuous touch with the simplicity of primitive society, furnish the forces dominating American character. The true point of view in the history of this nation is not the Atlantic coast, it is the Great West. Even the slavery struggle, which is made so exclusive an object of attention by writers like Professor von Holst, occupies its important place in American history because of its relation to westward expansion.

In this advance, the frontier is the outer edge of the wave—the meeting point between savagery and civilization. Much has been written about the frontier from the point of view of border warfare and the chase, but as a field for the serious study of the economist and the historian it has been neglected.

The American frontier is sharply distinguished from the European frontier—a fortified boundary line running through dense populations. The most significant thing about the American frontier is, that it lies at the hither edge of free land. In the census reports it is treated as the margin of that settlement which has a density of two or more to the square mile. The term is an elastic one, and for our purposes does not need sharp definition. We shall consider the whole frontier belt, including the Indian country and the outer margin of the "settled area" of the census reports. This paper will make no attempt to treat the subject exhaustively; its aim is simply to call attention to the frontier as a fertile field for investigation, and to suggest some of the problems which arise in connection with it.

In the settlement of America we have to observe how European life entered the continent, and how America modified and developed that life and reacted on Europe. Our early history is the study of European germs developing in an American environment. Too exclusive attention has been paid by institutional students to the Germanic origins, too little to the American factors. The frontier is the line of most rapid and effective Americanization. The wilderness masters the colonist. It finds him a European in dress, industries, tools, modes of travel, and thought. It takes him from the railroad car and puts him in the birch canoe. It strips off the garments of civilization and arrays him in the hunting shirt and the moccasin. It puts him in the log cabin of the Cherokee and Iroquois and runs an Indian palisade around him. Before long he has gone to planting Indian corn and plowing with a sharp stick; he shouts the war cry and takes the scalp in orthodox Indian fashion. In short, at the frontier the environment is at first too strong for the man. He must accept the conditions which it furnishes, or perish, and so he fits himself into the Indian clearings and follows the Indian trails. Little by little he transforms the wilderness, but the outcome is not the old Europe, not simply the development of Germanic germs, any more than the first phenomenon was a case of reversion to the Germanic mark. The fact is that here is a new product that is American. At first, the frontier was the Atlantic coast. It was the frontier of Europe in a very real sense. Moving westward, the frontier became more and more American. As successive terminal moraines result from successive glaciations, so each frontier leaves its traces behind it, and when it becomes a settled area the region still partakes of the frontier characteristics. Thus the advance of the frontier has meant a steady movement away from the influence of Europe, a steady growth of independence on American lines. And to study this advance, the men who grew up under these conditions, and the political, economic, and social results of it, is to study the really American part of our history.

In the course of the seventeenth century the frontier was advanced up the Atlantic river courses, just beyond the "fall line," and the tidewater region became the settled area. In the first half of the eighteenth century another advance occurred. Traders followed the Delaware and Shawnese Indians to the Ohio as early as the end of the first quarter of the century. Gov. Spotswood, of Virginia, made an expedition in 1714 across the Blue Ridge. The end of the first quarter of the century saw the advance of the Scotch-Irish and the Palatine Germans up the Shenandoah Valley into the western part of Virginia, and along the Piedmont region of the Carolinas. The Germans in New York pushed the frontier of settlement up the Mohawk to German Flats. In Pennsylvania the town of Bedford indicates the line of settlement. Settlements soon began on the New River, or the Great Kanawha, and on the sources of the Yadkin and French Broad. The King attempted to arrest the advance by his proclamation of 1763, forbidding settlements beyond the sources of the rivers flowing into the Atlantic; but in vain. In the period of the Revolution the frontier crossed the Alleghenies into Kentucky and Tennessee, and the upper waters of the Ohio were settled. When the first census was taken in 1790, the continuous settled area was bounded by a line which ran near the coast of Maine, and included New England except a portion of Vermont and New Hampshire, New York along the Hudson and up the Mohawk about Schenectady, eastern and southern Pennsylvania, Virginia well across the Shenandoah Valley, and the Carolinas and eastern Georgia. Beyond this region of continuous settlement were the small settled areas of Kentucky and Tennessee, and the Ohio, with the mountains intervening between them and the Atlantic area, thus giving a new and important character to the frontier. The isolation of the region increased its peculiarly American tendencies, and the need of transportation facilities to connect it with the East called out important schemes of internal improvement, which will be noted farther on. The "West," as a self-conscious section, began to evolve.

From decade to decade distinct advances of the frontier occurred. By the census of 1820 the settled area included Ohio, southern Indiana and Illinois, southeastern Missouri, and about one-half of Louisiana. This settled area had surrounded Indian areas, and the management of these tribes became an object of political concern. The frontier region of the time lay along the Great Lakes, where Astor's American Fur Company operated in the Indian trade, and beyond the Mississippi, where Indian traders extended their activity even to the Rocky Mountains; Florida also furnished frontier conditions. The Mississippi River region was the scene of typical frontier settlements.

The rising steam navigation on western waters, the opening of the Erie Canal, and the westward extension of cotton culture added five frontier states to the Union in this period. Grund, writing in 1836, declares: "It appears then that the universal disposition of Americans to emigrate to the western wilderness, in order to enlarge their dominion over inanimate nature, is the actual result of an expansive power which is inherent in them, and which by continually agitating all classes of society is constantly throwing a large portion of the whole population on the extreme confines of the State, in order to gain space for its development. Hardly is a new State or Territory formed before the same principle manifests itself again and gives rise to a further emigration; and so is it destined to go on until a physical barrier must finally obstruct its progress."

In the middle of this century the line indicated by the present eastern boundary of Indian Territory, Nebraska, and Kansas marked the frontier of the Indian country. Minnesota and Wisconsin still exhibited frontier conditions, but the distinctive frontier of the period is found in California, where the gold discoveries had sent a sudden tide of adventurous miners, and in Oregon, and the settlements in Utah. As the frontier had leaped over the Alleghenies, so now it skipped the Great Plains and the Rocky Mountains; and in the same way that the advance of the frontiersmen beyond the Alleghenies had caused the rise of important questions of transportation and internal improvement, so now the settlers beyond the Rocky Mountains needed means of communication with the East, and in the furnishing of these arose the settlement of the Great Plains and the development of still another kind of frontier life. Railroads, fostered by land grants, sent an increasing tide of immigrants into the Far West. The United States Army fought a series of Indian wars in Minnesota, Dakota, and the Indian Territory.

By 1880 the settled area had been pushed into northern Michigan, Wisconsin, and Minnesota, along Dakota rivers, and in the Black Hills region, and was ascending the rivers of Kansas and Nebraska. The development of mines in Colorado had drawn isolated frontier settlements into that region, and Montana and Idaho were receiving settlers. The frontier was found in these mining camps and the ranches of the Great Plains. The superintendent of the census for 1890 reports, as previously stated, that the settlements of the West lie so scattered over the region that there can no longer be said to be a frontier line.

In these successive frontiers we find natural boundary lines which have served to mark and to affect the characteristics of the frontiers, namely: the "fall line;" the Allegheny Mountains; the Mississippi; the Missouri where its direction approximates north and south; the line of the arid lands, approximately the ninety-ninth meridian; and the Rocky

Mountains. The fall line marked the frontier of the seventeenth century; the Alleghenies that of the eighteenth; the Mississippi that of the first quarter of the nineteenth; the Missouri that of the middle of this century (omitting the California movement); and the belt of the Rocky Mountains and the arid tract, the present frontier. Each was won by a series of Indian wars.

At the Atlantic frontier one can study the germs of processes repeated at each successive frontier. We have the complex European life sharply precipitated by the wilderness into the simplicity of primitive conditions. The first frontier had to meet its Indian question, its question of the disposition of the public domain, of the means of intercourse with older settlements, of the extension of political organization, of religious and educational activity. And the settlement of these and similar questions for one frontier served as a guide for the next. The American student needs not to go to the "prim little townships of Sleswick" for illustrations of the law of continuity and development. For example, he may study the origin of our land policies in the colonial land policy; he may see how the system grew by adapting the statutes to the custom of the successive frontiers. He may see how the mining experience in the lead regions of Wisconsin, Illinois, and Iowa was applied to the mining laws of the Sierras, and how our Indian policy has been a series of experimentations on successive frontiers. Each tier of new States has found in the older ones material for its constitutions. Each frontier has made similar contributions to American character, as will be discussed farther on.

But with all these similarities there are essential differences, due to the place element and the time element. It is evident that the farming frontier of the Mississippi Valley presents different conditions from the mining frontier of the Rocky Mountains. The frontier reached by the Pacific Railroad, surveyed into rectangles, guarded by the United States Army, and recruited by the daily immigrant ship, moves forward at a swifter pace and in a different way than the frontier reached by the birch canoe or the pack horse. The geologist traces patiently the shores of ancient seas, maps their areas, and compares the older and the newer. It would be a work worth the historian's labors to mark these various frontiers and in detail compare one with another. Not only would there result a more adequate conception of American development and characteristics, but invaluable additions would be made to the history of society.

Loria, the Italian economist, has urged the study of colonial life as an aid in understanding the stages of European development, affirming that colonial settlement is for economic science what the mountain is for geology, bringing to light primitive stratifications. "America," he says, "has the key to the historical enigma which Europe has sought for centuries in vain, and the land which has no history reveals luminously the course of universal history." There is much truth in this. The United States lies like a huge page in the history of society. Line by line as we read this continental page from West to East we find the record of social evolution. It begins with the Indian and the hunter; it goes on to tell of the disintegration of savagery by the entrance of the trader, the pathfinder of civilization; we read the annals of the pastoral stage in ranch life; the exploitation of the soil by the raising of unrotated crops of corn and wheat in sparsley settled farming communities; the intensive culture of the denser farm settlement; and finally the manufacturing organization with city and factory system. This page is familiar to the student of census statistics, but how little of it has been used by our historians. Particularly in eastern States this page is a palimpsest. What is now a manufacturing State was in an earlier decade an area of intensive farming. Earlier yet it had been a wheat area, and still earlier the "range" had attracted the cattleherder. Thus Wisconsin, now developing manufacture, is a State with varied agricultural interests. But earlier it was given over to almost exclusive grain-raising, like North Dakota at the present time.

Each of these areas has had an influence in our economic and political history; the evolution of each into a higher stage has worked political transformations. But what constitutional historian has made any adequate attempt to interpret political facts by the light of these social areas and changes? . . .

We may next inquire what were the influences on the East and on the Old World. A rapid enumeration of some of the more noteworthy effects is all that I have time for.

First, we note that the frontier promoted the formation of a composite nationality for the American people. The coast was preponderantly English, but the later tides of continental immigration flowed across to the free lands. This was the case from the early colonial days. The Scotch-Irish and the Palatine Germans, or "Pennsylvania Dutch," furnished the dominant element in the stock of the colonial frontier. With these peoples were also the freed indented servants, or redemptioners, who at the expiration of their time of service passed to the frontier. Governor Spotswood of Virginia writes in 1717, "The inhabitants of our frontiers are composed generally of such as have been transported hither as servants, and, being out of their time, settle themselves where land is to be taken up and that will produce the necessarys of life with little labour." Very generally these redemptioners were of non-English stock. In the crucible of the frontier the immigrants were Americanized, liberated, and fused into a mixed race, English in neither nationality nor characteristics. The process has gone on from the early days to our own. Burke and other writers in the middle of the eighteenth century believed that Pennsylvania was "threatened with the danger of being wholly foreign in language, manners, and perhaps even inclinations." The German and Scotch-Irish elements in the frontier of the South were only less great. In the middle of the present century the German element in Wisconsin was already so considerable that leading publicists looked to the creation of a German state out of the commonwealth by concentrating their colonization. Such examples teach us to beware of misinterpreting the fact that there is a common English speech in America into a belief that the stock is also English. . . .

From the conditions of frontier life came intellectual traits of profound importance. The works of travelers along each frontier from colonial days onward describe certain common traits, and these traits have, while softening down, still persisted as survivals in the place of their origin, even when a higher social organization succeeded. The result is that to the frontier the American intellect owes its striking characteristics. That coarseness and strength combined with acuteness and inquisitiveness; that practical, inventive turn of mind, quick to find expedients; that masterful grasp of material things, lacking in the artistic but powerful to effect great ends; that restless, nervous energy; that dominant individualism, working for good and for evil, and withal that buoyancy and exuberance which comes from freedom—these are traits of the frontier, or traits called out elsewhere because of the existence of the frontier. Since the days when the fleet of Columbus sailed into the waters of the New World, America has been another name for opportunity, and the people of the United States have taken their tone from the incessant expansion which has not only been open but has even been forced upon them. He would be a rash prophet who should assert that the expansive character of American life has now entirely ceased. Movement has been its dominant fact, and, unless this training has no effect upon a people, the American energy will continually demand a wider field for its excercise. But never again will such gifts of free land offer themselves. For a moment, at the frontier, the bonds of custom are broken and unrestraint is triumphant. There is not *tabula rasa.* The stubborn American environment is there with its imperious summons to accept its conditions; the inherited ways of doing things are also there; and yet, in spite of environment, and in spite of custom, each frontier did indeed furnish a new field of opportunity, a gate of escape from the bondage of the past; and freshness, and confidence, and scorn of older society, impatience of its restraints and its ideas, and indifference to its lessons, have accompanied the frontier. What the Mediterranean Sea was to the Greeks, breaking the bond of custom, offering new experiences, calling out new institutions and activities, that, and more, the ever retreating frontier has been to the United States directly, and to the nations of Europe more remotely. And now, four centuries from the discovery of America, at the end of a hundred years of life under the Constitution, the frontier has gone, and with its going has closed the first period of American history.

Half a century after Frederick Jackson Turner introduced his frontier hypothesis, WALTER PRESCOTT WEBB (1888–1963), late Professor of History at the University of Texas, expanded the frontier to include areas of Australia, Africa, and South America as well as North America. In *The Great Frontier* (1952) Webb finds an important dynamic element of our developing civilization has been the interaction between the "greater Wests" and the "little Easts." These environmental relationships have been the single most influential force affecting not only American life and institutions, but all western civilization.*

Walter Prescott Webb

Extension of the Frontier Principle

When Frederick Jackson Turner launched his frontier thesis, he must at times have wondered what the effect would be on his future reputation. Would it be more sensible to follow the tradition of his elders and glean the fields they had harvested, either substantiating their views of modifying them so little as not to disturb their sacred principles? His other choice was to strike out for himself and have a look at the country from a vantage point which others had not used. Though I am not an authority on Turner's life, I dare say he made his important decision not from considerations of policy, but because of an inner compulsion which drove him to make it regardless of the effect it might have on his career. A statesman has been described as a man who perceives a single truth of tomorrow. Occasionally there comes a historian who perceives an important truth of yesterday, discovers a set of relationships which throws a light on the past, and, if he sets it forth, and it is eventually accepted by a reasonable number of people, finds a place as an interpreter. No interpretation of history based on a general idea is ever universally accepted, and no interpreter escapes the tonic of criticism.

It would be bad taste for me to elaborate the basic idea that the frontier exerted a profound influence on American life, culture, and institutions. That idea is accepted and has by now pervaded all the fields of thought about this country.

*Reprinted from Walter Prescott Webb, "The Western World Frontier," in *The Frontier in Perspective*, Walker D. Wyman and Clifton B. Kroeber, editors, pp. 43–47, 1957, the University of Wisconsin Press. With permission of the copyright owners, the Regents of the University of Wisconsin.

That idea is permeating other lands similar to this, such as Canada, Australia, South Africa, and New Zealand. It is also being considered in the Latin-American countries to the south, and it will in the future be examined elsewhere.

I am submitting here what seems to me to be a truth of yesterday, an extension of the idea that the frontier exerted a far-reaching influence, not only on American life and institutions, but on all of Western civilization, and therefore on world history. The idea I am advancing is as simple as the one Turner announced and that others have elaborated. The American argument runs that there was for a long period a settled East and an unsettled West, a civilized region and a frontier region, that people were moving from the settled region into the unsettled one, that the process of moving and occupying raw land had its effects on those who moved, and that the whole long process had a reflex effect on the older region whence the people came. We may differ as to the extent of the influence, but it would require a strangely perverse mind to deny that there was some effect.

Here we have a principle of history demonstrated to be applicable in this country. It is gradually dawning on thinkers about other frontier countries that it is applicable in other countries too. If this principle of frontier influence is applicable in all the separate parts of the frontier, in Canada, Australia, South Africa, and New Zealand, in the twenty republics of Latin America, then this influence was exerted wherever the people of Western Europe took over frontier lands. In each of these countries there was in the beginning a little "East" and a greater "West." In each of them the little "East" ate into the greater "West," gradually reducing the West until in each country we can say there is no longer raw frontier. Also in each country, as in the United States, the process of eating up the frontier exerted influence on those who did the eating and had some reflex effect on those who did not participate. Thus, in each of the frontier countries, the scholars who have considered the frontier principle have followed the American lead and examined their own frontier as if it were an isolated example confined to their own country.

This limited procedure has been necessary and is invaluable. It was the method of Bacon, who believed that we should examine many details before inducing a general conclusion. This minute examination of the many little frontiers, little "Easts" and little "Wests," has resulted in the accumulation of a wealth of data about the processes that went on and has revealed a small central core of uniformity. The invasion of the little "West," the area of free land, has always had some effect on the little "East," on the civilization of that particular fragment.

The next step is to assemble all the little "Wests," all the fragments of the frontier, into the whole frontier, the greater "West," and when we have done this, we have a greater frontier than we have previously been examining; we have the whole instead of a parcel of parts of which the United States is only one. This whole Great Frontier originally would have comprised the three and one-half continents and the thousands of islands opened up by Columbus and his associates. This is a synthesis that was inevitable and is logical, once the idea of frontier has been accepted as a force in history.

But once we perform this act of synthesis and visualize all the scattered parts of the frontier brought together into a Great Frontier, we ask ourselves what of the little "Easts" and the little "Wests" with which we have been so concerned in such fragments as the United States and other dominions. We are for the moment looking at the whole frontier as analogous to the American West, thus merging the little "Easts" and the little "Wests" into one big "East." We have only lost—and that temporarily—the fragmentary "Easts," replicas of a greater "East," the existence of which has almost escaped notice. What we need look for now is the Mother East that gave birth to the little "Easts" tucked away on the fringes of the distant new lands. Our chief difficulty is psychological in that we have been concerned hitherto with the struggles and activities of the children and have lost sight of the home where the mother of all the little "Easts" resides. By an act of resolution, and at the expense perhaps of some preconceptions, we need to focus attention on the Mother East, which we can see by now is none other than Western Europe. Western Europe is the "East" in the American sense, bearing the same relation of the Great Frontier that the Atlantic Coast settlements long bore to the traditional American West. The name I have applied to Western Europe to set it off from the Great Frontier is the Metropolis. Since all of the frontier did not lie to the west of Europe, we must get away from our figurative use of East and West and substitute respectively the Metropolis and the Great Frontier. When we do this, we are in position to view the interaction and relation between the whole things rather than the relation between two parts—the civilized part and the frontier part—of a fragment of one of them only.

It is necessary for us to back away from the detail, the fragment, and have a fresh look at the *whole* Frontier and the *whole* Metropolis as they interacted on each other after 1500. There are advantages and disadvantages in shifting to this longer perspective and to this larger geographical canvas.

The disadvantages are: Since the whole frontier is greater than any of its parts, so the task of thinking about it is of greater scope and magnitude. The whole frontier is a complex thing, varying with the varied geography and dissimilar people, whereas a single frontier has both geographic unity and a measure of cultural unity. It is difficult for one person to know all the lands and the languages and literatures, but he who shrinks from difficulties should not elect to be a historian.

It would seem that the advantages of taking the long perspective and looking at the whole frontier instead of a part of it overbalance the difficulties. The fundamental gain derived from the long perspective and the world view is this: It enables us to see the whole, the Great Frontier on the one hand and the whole of Metropolis on the other. We see the extent of the forest, its relation to what is around it, and we see over the centuries the people of the Metropolis moving out on it, nibbling tentatively at its edges along the Atlantic seaboard, upward from the Cape, inward from Sydney and Melbourne, and inward from the South American shore. From all these points, the migrating hordes from the Metropolis move in rough unison on the forest and the plain, and eventually they claim a simultaneous victory on a broad intercontinental field because they have destroyed that which so challenged and lured them.

When we view this interaction from this high vantage point, things seem to fall into place. What in closer perspective appeared as separate and disconnected historical phenomena now appear as scattered manifestations of a single action. For example, I mentioned the little "Easts" and the little "Wests" with which we have been so busy. We now see that they are cut of the same two cloths. The little "Easts" are but extended fingers of the Metropolis; the little "Wests" are what is left in various places of the original Great Frontier.

When from this same vantage point we observe the interaction between the Metropolis and the Great Frontier over a period of four and one-half centuries, we feel that we have perhaps found one of the important keys to modern Western civilization. In this interaction, we see a prime example of Toynbee's challenge and response; we see a backdrop of Spengler's philosophy of rise and decay, which he probably did not see. This interaction between these two gigantic forces developed so much power that, like a diesel engine, it picked up all the other historical movements, such as the price revolution, the commercial revolution, the industrial revolution, and the democratic revolutions, and moved them like a long train down the track. Whatever got in the way of this interaction was altered or destroyed; whatever harmonized with it or served it, prospered. In the long perspective, both capitalism and democracy appear as by-products of the interaction, the use of the precious metals as a medium of exchange appears as an episode now ended, and the rise of modern Negro slavery appears as a device adopted by the Metropolitans in order that they might have cheap and permanent labor with which to hew their fortunes out of the raw materials of the Great Frontier. Before this interaction, the old ideas about economics, based on scarcity, were wrecked because they were not applicable to the new age of plenty. Mercantilism gave way to lassez faire, which lasted only as long as the frontier lasted. These are some of the vistas that open up when we view the whole Frontier and its relation to the whole Metropolis, vistas which cannot ordinarily be reached by the most minute examination of a single frontier fragment.

If the frontier environment did create new opportunities for the pioneers and provide a place for ideas to be tried, still it was the source of neither the pioneer's ambition nor the ideas with which he lived. CARL N. DEGLER (b. 1921), Professor of History at Vassar College, counters the Turner thesis, arguing that Turner underestimated the lasting conservative qualities of men's cultural patterns. But Degler does suggest that the popular belief in the frontier as a place of opportunity undoubtedly made it an important influence upon the attitudes and character of the people.*

Carl N. Degler

Does Land Mold Character?

"So vast is the Territory of North America," prophesied Benjamin Franklin in 1751, "that it will require many Ages to settle it fully; and, till it is fully settled, Labour will never be cheap here, where no Man continues long a Labourer for others, but gets a Plantation of his own. . . ." Franklin's observations on the impact of empty land upon Americans was echoed by many another American in his time and later: Jefferson, Hamilton, Emerson, and Henry George are only some of the older ones. The conviction that the roots of the American character are to be found in the frontier experience has long since passed into the folk wisdom of the nation, and in our own century it has been a stock in trade of historical scholars as well.

In the waning years of the nineteenth century, the vague belief that, in some fashion or other, the frontier was a formative factor in the history of the United States was boldly cast into an academic hypothesis by a young historian from the West. The study of American history has not been the same since Frederick Jackson Turner made that presentation before the American Historical Association in 1893; only Charles A. Beard has exercised a comparable influence upon the writing of our history.

This influence has stemmed primarily from Turner's broad, but highly suggestive and challenging thesis, running all through his writings, that the settling of a new land did more to mold the character of the American people and institu-

*From pp. 123–135 in *Out of Our Past* by Carl N. Degler, Copyright © 1959 by Carl N. Degler. Reprinted by permission of Harper & Row, Publishers. Footnote omitted.

tions than the European heritage. "American democracy was born of no theorist's dream," he argued in one essay, "it was not carried in the *Susan Constant* to Virginia, nor in the *Mayflower* to Plymouth. It came out of the American forest, and it gained new strength each time it touched a new frontier. Not the constitution," he asserted, "but free land, and an abundance of natural resources open to a fit people, made the democratic type of society in America. . . ." Furthermore, something more than democracy issued from the forest; "the frontier," he contended, "is productive of individualism" in the American character. In his first and most famous frontier essay, he concluded "that to the frontier the American intellect owes its striking characteristics."

As a number of scholars have subsequently pointed out, Turner was generous in attributing a variety of American traits to the frontier, but it is not always clear what he meant by the frontier. Sometimes, in Turner's writings, it is an area—that is, the zone where civilization and forest meet; at other times the frontier is little more than the western part of the United States, although it is obvious that Illinois in 1850 is hardly a zone of contact between civilization and savagery. At still other places in his writings Turner is apparently thinking of the frontier as a process—a way of life for those actually participating in the settling of vacant lands. Then, at another time, he will write of the frontier as an abundance of natural resources. As analytical tools for explaining the origins of Americans, these four definitions are of quite different orders. To lump them under the single heading of the "influence of the frontier" is to obscure rather than to clarify. "As an analytical device," Richard Hofstadter has said, the frontier thesis "was a blunt instrument." If the frontier is the cutting edge of civilization, then it clearly cannot also be the western part of the United States at a later stage of social evolution; and if it is natural resources, then it is not the process of settlement, for men may wrestle with the problems of subduing a wilderness but enjoy only a paucity of natural resources. In short, these four definitions of the same term are not only different; they are sometimes mutually exclusive.

Turner never tired of reiterating that the frontier remade the Europeans who entered it. "The wilderness masters the colonist," he explained. "It finds him a European in dress, industries, tools, modes of travel, and thought. . . . It strips off the garments of civilization and arrays him in the hunting shirt and the moccasin. It puts him in the log cabin of the Cherokee and Iroquois and runs an Indian palisade around him. . . . In short, at the frontier the environment is at first too strong for the man." But after the first adjustment, the pioneer begins to change. "Little by little he transforms the wilderness, but the outcome is not the old Europe. . . . The fact is, that here is a new product that is American." This was a most persuasive argument, but Turner was so imbued with a belief in the influence of environment that he underestimated the tough conservative character of men's cultural patterns.

Sixty years before Turner, Alexis de Tocqueville believed, much the same as Turner, that in America one could actually witness the successive stages of social evolution. Upon visiting the actual frontier of Michigan, however, Tocqueville found that his assumption required serious modification. "Of all the countries of the world America is the least fitted to furnish the spectacle I came there to seek," he noted in his diary. "In America, even more than in Europe there is only one society. . . . The plane of a uniform civilization has passed over it. The man you left behind in New-York you find again in almost impenetrable solitudes: same clothes, same attitude, same language, same habits, same pleasures." To factors like widespread education, "the spirit of equality," and the very recent contact with civilized living Tocqueville attributed the "universal civilization" in America. The settlers on the Michigan frontier, he wrote, "have come with the customs, the ideas, the needs of civilization. They only yield to savagery that which the imperious necessity of things exacts from them. . . ." Tocqueville then described a cabin, deep in the virtually untouched forest, at which he visited. But, he said, if you think you are entering the abode of the American peasant, you are wrong. "You enter this cabin which seems the asylum of all the miseries, but the owner wears the same clothes as you, he speaks the language of the cities. On his rude table are books and newspapers"; he asks about events in Europe. In fact, "the wood cabin is only a temporary refuge for the American, a temporary concession made to the exigencies of the situation." As soon as possible he will reproduce his civilized life as he knew it, right in the midst of the wilderness.

Tocqueville, the observer, is a better guide to the cultural impact of the frontier than Turner, the historian. Instead of recapitulating the cultural history of the race, men on the frontier did their best to reproduce the civilization as quickly as they could when they came. More recently, Louis B. Wright, in his book *Culture on the Moving Frontier,* has shown in some detail how this was done through the seventeenth, eighteenth, and nineteenth centuries.

The most widely accepted part of Turner's frontier hypothesis is that American democracy is a unique product of the struggle with the wilderness. One of the favorite means for substantiating this point has been to point to the democratic features of the western state constitutions. Universal manhood suffrage, elected officials, and so forth, it is argued, first appeared in the western states and then spread to the rest of America. Actually, however, as one of Turner's disciples, John Barnhart, has recently shown, the constitutions of Kentucky and Tennessee—the first transmontane states to enter the Union—were both modeled after the Pennsylvania Constitution of 1790—a document which was considerably more conservative than the 1776 organic law of that state! Rarely, as Barnhart demonstrates, did these western states, for all their supposed democratic propensities, make a novel contribution to government; they merely copied from the eastern states.

From his investigations of the provisions of the state constitutions of the Ohio-Mississippi region—the so-called "Valley of Democracy"—Barnhart found only a handful of clauses which could be called original with the West. In Ohio's first constitutions, for example, out of 106 clauses, only eleven were counted as original, while fifty were very much like those in Tennessee's and nineteen like those in Pennsylvania's. Lest this be thought to be an instance of one "advanced democratic" western state copying from another, it should be noted that forty-seven of Tennessee's clauses were taken from the constitution of Pennsylvania and nineteen from North Carolina's.

To be sure, as one looks over the constitutions of the states in the first half of the nineteenth century, it is clear that democratic forms came earlier, on the average, to the new states than to the old. But since it can also be shown that an old state like Pennsylvania in 1776 wrote a constitution more radically democratic than those of most western states in subsequent years, it does not appear that democracy is uniquely a product of the West, much less of the forest.

Moreover, if we broaden our perspective a little, we cannot escape noticing that the most democratic ideas expressed anywhere in European civilization before the nineteenth century were those of the Levellers in seventeenth-century England. No one has argued, however, that their demand for universal manhood suffrage and a written constitution to protect the people against arbitrary government was a result of the frontier.

But the failure of the Levellers to gain their democratic objectives, while the pioneers in the American forest secured theirs, suggests that the influence of the frontier lay not in its evocation of democratic ideas, but in the providing of an opportunity for them to be put into practice regardless of their place or occasion of origin. This would explain why democratic forms seemed to come more slowly to eastern states than to western; the latter had a clean slate on which to write new ideas. Though Turner seems to have underestimated the conservative streak which makes men strive to perpetuate the old in the midst of the new environment, he nevertheless grasped the important fact that ideas and innovations unable to get a trial in the older states often were put into practice in the communities abuilding in the West.

Such a function of the frontier, though not as formative as Turner asserted, is still important. Free land offered a chance for political and social experiment by peaceful means, and this opportunity unquestionably aided the rapid triumph of democratic ideals in America. But to repeat, the availability of opportunity should not be confused with the origination of democratic ideas. Later, by looking at the experiences of other peoples who were confronted with frontiers of empty land, we shall see that empty land does not always produce democracy or liberty.

But there is more to be said about the democratic influence of the frontier. Recently, two scholars, Eric McKitrick and Stanley Elkins, have suggested that Turner's accent on the frontier as the molder of American democracy has been not so much misplaced as merely inexpertly elucidated. They decry, to begin with, the excessive emphasis by Turner's critics upon formal definitions of democracy, such as suffrage qualifications, constitutional provisions, and the like. McKitrick and Elkins would substitute a functional definition of American democracy in which the essence is taken to be concern with political problems and the active participation in community affairs on the part of large numbers of citizens. Under this definition, they point out, the newness of the land, the necessity of establishing brand-new communities in the wilderness, demanded greater participation in political activity than was true in Europe. Therefore, they say, the empty land may be said to have contributed to the making of a peculiarly American variety of democracy.

Moreover, with so much to be done in the raw communities of the West, there simply were not enough trained and traditionally accepted leaders to organize and manage the new settlements. Hence ordinary people, Everyman, had to come forward and pitch in. As this procedure was repeated across the face of the land, the habit of community problem solving, to use the phraseology of McKitrick and Elkins, became fixed in the American character. From this, they think, stemmed the American propensity for associative activity, committee forming, writing of petitions, and the general recourse to political and group action. This conception of the frontier is close to Turner's; but because it does not suffer from his confusion of definitions for the frontier, it is much more convincing.

The participation of many people in the affairs of government, McKitrick and Elkins further point out, inevitably reinforces self-confidence and self-reliance —qualities usually associated with the frontier and the American. How the new land did this economically was illustrated by Karl Marx in the latter part of the nineteenth century. Marx's example was a letter written by a French worker who went to California. "I never could have believed," the worker wrote, "that I was capable of working at the various occupations I was employed on in California. I was firmly convinced that I was fit for nothing but letter press printing. . . ." But once "in the midst of this world of adventurers, who change their occupation as often as they do their shirt, egad, I did as the others. As mining did not turn out remunerative enough, I left it for the town, where in succession I became a typographer, a slater, plumber, etc. In consequence of thus finding out that I am fit for any sort of work, I feel less of a mollusk and more of a man."

One must be careful, however, not to romanticize the opportunities of the free land to the point of unreality. Both Turner and his followers, for example, have written of the West as a safety valve for the unsuccessful and discontented of the East. So plausible has this hypothesis appeared that laymen and academic historians alike talk of the significance for American society of the "closing" of the frontier in 1890.

But, suggestive as the safety-valve theory is, it, too, like the thesis of the frontier origins of American democracy, suffers when subjected to close analysis. For example, of the large number of historians who have undertaken concrete examinations of the validity of this thesis, almost none has found evidence that discontented and poor urban workers of the East could find a second chance in the West of the nineteenth century. Two economic historians tried to uncover examples of workers who left an industrial town like Fall River, Massachusetts, for new opportunities in the West; but, though they combed newspaper after newspaper, they found no evidence of emigrating workers. Another historian demonstrated that the cost of starting a farm in the West in the nineteenth century was in excess of a year and a half's income of the average urban worker if he was fortunate enough to work all year. Confirmation of the urban worker's inability to finance his own movement to the West was forthcoming in another study which reported that, during the 1850's in New York City, societies were formed to assist workers to make the trip to the hinterland. By implication this was evidence that few workers were in a position to leave for the West on their own. Finally, in what he called a "post-mortem" on the safety-valve thesis, Fred Shannon noted that the census, especially after the Civil War, clearly showed that the largest migration of Americans was from the country to the city and not the other way around, as the safety-valve hypothesis would have it.

Yet despite the avalanche of attack, adverse evidence, and the paucity of defensive data, something is still to be salvaged from this much-mauled thesis of Turner. Shannon, resting his case on the census data, has vehemently argued that, rather than the country's being a safety valve for the discontent of the city, the urban centers were the outlet for farm discontent and surplus population. Such an argument is going too far, however. The very existence of an empty frontier, which in the course of the years was gradually populated, makes it obvious that pressure on the city was reduced to the extent that some people—especially farmers and new immigrants—went to western farming areas instead of to the city. In this *indirect* sense, one is justified in talking about the ameliorative effect of the frontier on urban crowding and in preserving opportunities for city workers. Nor should it be forgotten, though little research has been done on this aspect of the problem, that the West—though not the frontier—had cities; many craftsmen and small shop owners must have migrated from the highly competitive and overcrowded cities of the East to seek new opportunities in the towns of the West.

The fact remains, however, that once tests of data are applied to it, the safety-valve thesis in any literal sense does not come off very well. Not many eastern people in the nineteenth century could actually utilize the West as a safety valve for their discontent or as an opportunity for a new start.

But to confine our analysis of the impact of the West on America to measurable matters is to miss the tremendous psychological import of the safety-valve conception. All through the nineteenth century, Americans believed that the West was a haven for the oppressed and a cornucopia for the ambitious. This was the underlying reason for the liberalizing of the land laws in the course of the century. George Henry Evans and his Land Reformers, Thomas Hart Benton and his Pre-emption Act, Andrew Johnson's and the Republican party's homestead bills, all epitomized the belief that if the lands of the West were made easy of acquisition, "every worker will be enabled to hew out for his family a home from the virgin soil of the Great West," as Horace Greeley put it in 1859. A form of this conviction lay behind the efforts on the part of businessmen and philanthropists in the 1850's to organize societies to help defray the expenses of the unemployed in traveling to the western lands. During the Panic of 1857, newspapers constantly urged the unemployed to go West for work. "It should be known to females out of employment," counseled a Philadelphia newspaper in 1857, "that throughout the West, there are thousands of homes and liberal pay awaiting any reputable persons who are willing to engage themselves for domestic duties." The Children's Aid Society of New York, under the imaginative and energetic leadership of Charles Loring Brace, undertook a continuous program of sending homeless children to the West. Between 1853 and 1872 some twenty thousand New York City children were placed in homes in the West. The Association for the Improvement of the Condition of the Poor, in 1858, though hostile to the idea of aided emigration for urban workers, nevertheless conceded that "The relief of our overburdened city of its pauperism, by migration to the country is a very popular idea. . . ."

And precisely because it was *believed* to be a safety valve, regardless of what it was in fact, the western frontier worked an influence upon the attitudes of Americans. It left its mark in the optimism, the belief in progress, the promise of the future and the second chance—all of which have been deeply embedded in the American character.

The influence of the doctrine is seen also in the widespread acceptance of the corollary that the closing of the frontier meant the end of an older America. "Our last frontier has long since been reached," Franklin Roosevelt said in 1932, "and there is practically no more free land. . . . There is no safety valve in the form of a western prairies to which those thrown out of work by the eastern machines can go for a new start." The view that the ending of the frontier posed new problems for the American economy found easy acceptance among a group of prominent and influential economists in the 1930's. For them the economy had lost its motive power when the frontier closed. "The Bogy of Economic Maturity," as one of their opponents phrased it, gripped a whole generation of depression economists, of whom Alvin Hansen of Harvard was the chief. These men found in the depression the final confirmation of the effects of the end of the frontier in 1890. They asked, as Hansen put it in the title of one of his books, "Stagnation or Recovery?" Only through government investment, they argued, could the natural stagnation of the economy now be overcome.

Generally, of course, these economists drew upon John Maynard Keynes for their economics, but their historical frame of reference was the work of Frederick Jackson Turner. In the remarkably widespread acceptance of the frontier hypothesis among men of affairs and humble citizens alike is a striking vindication of Lord Keynes' remark that ideas, whether right or wrong, can exert enormous social influence. As a psychological force the frontier has not yet lost its power; it is still common coin in American thought. Certainly while the frontier was in being, it was powerful in fostering the belief that the American was unique and different from the European. And insofar as he believed so, he was.

Underlying most of the criticisms of Turner is the assumption that the frontier influence is in reality passive rather than active. When Turner's thesis, which is essentially a geographical interpretation of history, is cut to its marrow, it stands forth as the simple assertion that when people move into a new geographical setting they alter their mores. This proposition has been amply documented and repeatedly demonstrated for a variety of environments. An especially convincing example is *The Great Plains,* by Walter Prescott Webb, a disciple of Turner's. But even in Webb's study it is apparent that geography is less a creator of culture and more a selector of existent cultural patterns. Men found it difficult to continue to be wheat farmers when climatic and soil conditions were more suited to cattle raising. But the cattle business did not spring forth for the first time on the Great Plains—it merely flourished there after being introduced from other areas. Climate and soil prevented New England from being a cotton-producing area, but they did not dictate that Maine should grow potatoes. Geography may set the limits within which men must live, but it does not determine which of several alternatives available to man's cultural versatility actually will be pursued.

The best proof of this generalization in regard to the frontier theory can be found in an examination of the effects of empty land upon peoples other than Americans. Several peoples of the world, both in the remote and recent past, have had to wrestle with the challenge of a raw frontier. In the twelfth century, the area east of the Elbe River constituted a nearly empty frontier land for the restless Saxons of north Germany. The movement of Germans into this region was one of the great colonizing efforts of the Middle Ages; and in some respects, this frontier wrought changes in the customs of the Saxons who settled on the vacant lands.

The form of village settlement, for example, changed strikingly. Serfdom declined and its burdens were considerably lightened as lords were compelled to recognize that the peasants had access to more land and opportunity to the east. Though undoubtedly there were changes in cultural patterns, they were already implicit in the old ways; they merely awaited an opportunity for expression, just as the liberalizing of franchise requirements in the western United States waited upon the opportunity of a new land for realization. In sum, the empty land in Germany determined neither the direction the changes would take nor the character of them.

This is illustrated even more clearly if one compares the alleged effects of the frontier upon the character of Americans and the South African Boers. The history of both peoples is dominated by the movement into open land. There can be no question of the fierce individualism and the hatred of outside control which characterize the typical cattle-raising Boer, but his almost fanatical conservatism in matters of religion, science, education, and government are in sharp contrast with the belief in progress, education, science and liberal government which has always stood out in the complex of American national traits. Both peoples struggled with the demands of the empty lands in which they settled, but the resulting traits and cultural patterns were strikingly different because each brought its own cultural baggage into the more or less neutral frontier. New land denies vitality to certain cultural patterns, but it creates no particular ones.

One other frontier experience might be mentioned. Like the Americans, the Russians of the eighteenth and nineteenth centuries were a people constantly in contact with a frontier. While the Americans were moving west, the Russians were striking east across Russia and Siberia. Both peoples reached their respective Pacific shores about the same time. Here, however, the similarity stops; movement into the steppes of southern Russia and into Siberia by a people governed by an autocrat brought no liberalization of the regime, nor did it prepare the ground for a democratic society. The Cossacks of the lower Don, it is true, came into being as a people in the seventeenth century while in direct contact with the free lands of the region, and enjoyed for a while a primitive democratic military organization. But it was not long, despite the frontier, before an oligarchy emerged, slowly but ineluctably changing the Cossacks into the most reactionary arm of the czarist regime. It is hard to find among the Cossacks any signs of the frontier influence of democracy and individualism as Turner spoke of it in America. Once again the cultural patterns of each people remained largely unchanged even though both peoples moved into an area of empty land.

Old cultural traits persisted on the American frontier. One scholar has found that when Germans in colonial America moved into Pennsylvania, Maryland, and Virginia, they differed markedly from the English colonists in farming methods, crops, and labor system. The Germans selected clay loams in heavily wooded areas, while the English chose light, sandy uplands. Whereas the English girdled trees and farmed among the stumps, the fastidious Germans cleared the land completely and plowed deeply. The English, on the other hand, merely scratched the soil and were appalled to see it run away in the rains. Tidewater Virginians let their stock roam freely, but the careful Germans actually built their barns before they built homes. Unlike the English, the conservative Germans did not take to tobacco cultivation, but stuck to the familiar wheat; nor did they become slaveholders as avidly as the English. Both peoples were on the same frontier, but the vacant land did little more than provide them with a canvas upon which each depicted the old familiar cultural patterns. In his enthusiastic conception of the frontier as a democratizing force, Turner ignored the new lease on life given to slavery by the free land of the West. Though the new southern states in the early years of the nineteenth century accurately reflected in their constitutions the national trend toward greater popular participation in government, these same constitutions were conspicuous for their complete acceptance of human slavery at the very time the institution was more and more viewed as contrary to the democratic spirit.

It is apparent from any survey of frontiers throughout the world that free land offers opportunities for social advancement and wealth accumulation. But whether men will seize these opportunities often depends more upon the cultural attitudes they bring with them than upon the free land. The land, in and of itself, will not do it. The history of the Indians and the Spaniards on the American frontier is a case in point here. The availability of free land and natural resources did not spur them on to new forms of production because their cultural heritage did not include the traits which fostered such activity. But bring into this empty land the work-conscious Puritan, for instance, and then the free land takes on a different aspect; it now becomes a spur, a veritable goad to economic activity and hard work. Similarly, a people with a vigorous conception of self-government, moving into new lands, finds it natural to expand popular participation in government, as McKitrick and Elkins have shown occurred on the American frontier. But it is important to recognize that it is not the land which makes the difference; it is the cultural attitudes of the people. The frontier, rather than being the key to American development, is merely one among a number of influences which have gone into the shaping of Americans.

RAY ALLEN BILLINGTON (b. 1903) received the Ph.D. degree at Harvard University in 1933. Since 1963 he has been a Senior Research Associate on the staff of the Huntington Library. He has written many books on the West, including *Westward Expansion* (1949) and *The Far Western Frontier: 1830–1860* (1956). *America's Frontier Heritage* (1967), from which this essay is taken, represents Billington's synthesis of all frontier scholarship over a sixty-year period. He argues thoroughly and conclusively that the social environment made a lasting imprint upon the American character.*

Ray Allen Billington

The Frontier Social Environment as Key

If the hundreds of visitors from overseas who have written about the United States can be believed, we Americans are a strange and inexplicable lot. We work too hard; even our games are played with a grim determination to have a good time. We are forever moving about, showing none of the attachment to place and family of normal human beings. We rebel against tradition, even to experimenting with the new when the old is still useful. We are shockingly wasteful, addicted to such extravagances as disposable tissues, throw-away beer cans, and automobiles cunningly contrived to wear out after a few years of use. We venerate our wives, shower them with adulation, burden them with authority, and reduce the mere male to a henpecked nonentity. We are crassly materialistic, absorbed in pursuing the Almighty Dollar, and blind to cultural values. We are so unrealistically optimistic that we would refuse to recognize the day of doom were its shadow already upon us.

A few more astute visitors—those probing beneath the surface behavior to explore that mystical ethos known as a "national character"—have added to this list of particulars. Americans, they say, display a naive nationalism; they magnify minor incidents into wars (as they did the unpleasantness in Korea in 1950), and they flex their military muscles whenever another nation indulges in a bit of diplomatic bluffing (as did Russia in an

*Excerpts from *America's Frontier Heritage* by Ray Allen Billington. Copyright © 1966 by Ray Allen Billington. Reprinted by permission of Holt, Rinehart and Winston, Inc., pp. 1–3, 46–50, 52–54, 58–60, 61–64, 66–68.

annoying number of cases during the Cold War). Americans have been and are wedded to a brand of "rugged individualism" already proved obsolescent in the urban-industrial world of the twentieth century. And Americans, they argue, have such an emotional attachment to democracy that they refuse to see virtue in any other form of government, encourage those of humblest birth to become Presidents, and call servants "gentlemen" and masters "hey you."

Putting aside for the moment the truth or falsity of these appraisals, the fact remains that a good many hundred travelers have isolated these traits as peculiarly American; so many, indeed, that their chorus of assent becomes convincing. We Americans do exhibit characteristics not shared by our cousins beyond the seas. This does not mean that we are the sole owners of an entirely unique character; many "uniquely" American traits are exhibited elsewhere in the western world today as mounting prosperity encourages mobility, democracy, optimism, materialism, and even a touch of wastefulness. It does mean that over the past two centuries European visitors have found those characteristics so exaggerated in the United States that they have branded Americans a different people. The Londoner who remarks, as many have, that he feels more at home in Paris than Chicago is only mirroring a belief that the Americans have been transmuted into a different species from the English pioneers who planted their civilization at Jamestown and Plymouth three centuries ago.

Why this transmutation? Historians have proposed a number of answers, all more or less true. Some have gone so far as to deny that differences exist, and have argued learnedly if ineffectively that man's character is unchangeable. Others have ascribed uniquely American traits to the ethnic hodgepodge created by immigration; they dwell on the effect of acculturation and on the results of borrowing from many cultures. Still others see American distinctiveness as a by-product of the nation's abundant natural resources or of the physical mobility that keeps the people forever on the move. That there is a kernel of truth in each of these explanations is indisputable. Historians have long realized that events occur and characteristics emerge through the operation of many forces; human behavior is too infinitely complex to be explained by any single cause. We must visualize the distinctive features of American civilization as the product of the multitudinous forces contributing to the country's heritage.

To this list, however, one more must be added, and this book will argue that it has been of major importance. It will maintain that some—but by no means all—of the characteristics that Europeans brand uniquely American were the product of the three centuries of pioneering needed to settle the continent. It will defend what scholars call the "frontier hypothesis."

This hypothesis may be stated thus: The Europeans who founded the New World settlements in the seventeenth century and the later pioneers who were lured ever westward by the thirst for furs or cheap land or gold or adventure found themselves in an unfamiliar environment. In Europe and the East men were many and land was scarce; on the frontiers men were few and land was abundant. There the old laws governing compact societies no longer applied. Traditional techniques of production were unsuited to an environment where resources were more plentiful than manpower; innovation and experimentation became a way of life. Attachment to place diminished in a land where more attractive places lay ahead; mobility came to be a habit. Pinchpenny Easterners so profited by exploiting nature's abundance that their thrifty ways were outmoded; wastefulness was a natural consequence. Cultural creativity lost its appeal to men burdened with the task of clearing a continent; materialism emerged as a desirable creed no less than an economic necessity. Leisure was nonexistent in frontier communities; hard work became a persistent habit. Inherited titles seemed archaic and traditional class distinctions less meaningful in a land where a man's worth to society was judged by his own skills; a democratic social system with greater possibilities for upward mobility followed naturally. And, most important of all, men found that the man-land ratio on the frontier provided so much opportunity for the individual to better himself that external controls were not necessary; individualism and political democracy were enshrined as their ideals. These were the traits which were revitalized over and over again as the frontier moved westward, eventually creating an American way of life and thought that was distinct.

This is the argument of those who uphold the "frontier hypothesis" as one—but only one—of the several forces shaping the civilization of the United States. . . .

Clearly the frontier was not simply a line drawn exactly across a map. It was a broad zone in which men with countless skills labored to exploit virgin riches. It was, moreover, a migrating region, moving westward at a rate of from ten to forty miles each year. At times, when a natural or Indian barrier lay ahead, it might contract as it did in the eighteenth century when the shock troops of expansion were held back by the Appalachian Mountains and the French with their Indian allies. At others it might broaden, as in the 1830s and 1840s when its advance agents ranged a thousand miles beyond the frontier of farms and towns in the Mississippi Valley. Yet always this zone did migrate, and always it provided a haven for men who sought opportunity in newness.

Let us indulge in a thoroughly unhistorical speculation. Suppose that in the year A.D. 752 the emperor Hsüan Tsung, wearying of the brilliant scholars in his Academy of Letters and moved by the plight of his overcrowded peasantry, decided to dispatch his most experienced navigator, Bo Ko Lum, to search for a route to thinly settled Europe. Assume that Bo Ko Lum, sailing eastward with three sturdy ships, made his landfall in a gentle country that he mistook for a remote outpost of the Frankish kingdom where he was welcomed by friendly natives called, by the Chinese, Red Franks. Pretend that this newly discovered continent, later called Frankland, was occupied over the next century by hundreds of thousands of settlers from China's overpopulated mainland. They would fashion rice paddies, build their pagodas to worship at the shrine of Buddha, and slowly advance their Asiatic civilization eastward, led by venturesome fur trappers in flowing silken robes. As they moved ever onward toward the rising sun until they reached the distant Atlantic they would leave behind a new Orient, transplanted across the seas, and modeled after the Orient they had left behind.

But would this civilization be an exact replica of the old? It would not. Chinese pioneers would discover that silken robes were less resistant to wilderness wear than jackets and pantaloons of hides, that corn and wheat were more easily produced than rice, and that decrees of a distant emperor were easily ignored by a people whose unique problems demanded unique local solutions. They would, over the course of years, change in appearance, in dietary habits, and in social values as the wilderness of Frankland altered their customs and institutions. A future Chinese historian might write that they had been Franklandized by the New World environment. Yet would this transformation convert the colonists into replicas of the pioneers who actually settled the West? Certainly not. Transplanted cultural patterns would be too powerful to be completely submerged. The imaginary Frankland as an outpost of China would have borne little resemblance to the actual America as an outpost of England. But it would also show little similarity to the China from which the settlers had come.

This imagined situation brings into focus the basic question that must be answered if we are to appraise the influence of the frontier on American civilization. Can a culture be basically altered by transplantation to a different physical environment? And, if it can, how is this accomplished? To solve these problems we must weigh the relative influence of traditional cultural forces and the physical environment in shaping group cultures.

Geneticists have learned a great deal about the hereditary process. They know that traits are transmitted from parents to children through the forty-six chromosomes present in every fertilized ovum, that these chromosomes are made up of complex molecules called "genes," and that these genes are reshuffled from generation to generation, giving rise to the endless new combinations that relieve us of the unpleasant necessity of all looking alike. They also know that hereditary traits are rigidly restrained (save in the rare case of mutations) and that they are passed along by the genes from generation to generation utterly unchanged by life experiences. This means that *learned* skills or experiences cannot be inherited; we inherit only a certain physical structure, intelligence, temperament, and innate drives.

Environment plays an equally important role in shaping our behavior. Actually we are influenced by two interacting environments, the "primary" or *physical* environment that comprises the world of nature about us, and the "secondary" or *social* environment provided by the human group in which we find ourselves. Of these two, the latter is more immediately important, for the social group serves as a medium through which primary environmental forces reach the individual; its influence operates within limits set by the physical environment but within these limits it plays a transcendent role. Each group has its own patterns of behavior known as a *culture,* which include the shared knowledge, beliefs, customs, and habits that have been acquired by living together over the course of generations. These "cultures" vary from group to group and account for many of the differences that distinguish peoples; they determine the nature of the skills that we acquire, the knowledge that we accumulate, the basic assumptions that we hold, and the conscious or unconscious values that govern our behavior. This means that each group has its own social environment that affects the behavior of those within the group.

The culture of any people tends to change constantly as traditional practices are eliminated and adjustments made to meet new situations. In a forming social order these changes occur frequently as the group adjusts itself to its physical environment, accustoms itself to surrounding peoples, and experiments with behavior patterns. Once established, however, these patterns tend to perpetuate themselves; although change continues, the rate of change slows as each society tends to regard its culture as proper and to resist further alteration. At this point in social evolution the group is a victim of ethnocentrism.

Thus man's social behavior is influenced by both heredity and environment. Inherited characteristics are passed from generation to generation and change so slowly as the evolutionary process operates that differences are not observable within historical periods; they are unaffected by experience, although modes of expression may be altered by cultural change. Environment is both physical and social, with the latter more determinative of social behavior within limits set by the former. Central to the social environment is the "culture" of each group. This emerges in the early stages of social organization and while changing constantly to adapt to changing conditions—in the physical environment, technology, ethnic variation, and the like—tends to solidify and to be increasingly resistant to change as ethnocentrism becomes a factor. Such changes as do occur after this point result from continuing alterations in the physical environment and from interaction with adjacent cultures that mutually influence each other.

Against this background of established theory, we can ask three questions essential to understanding the frontier process: Is the behavior pattern of the individual altered by changes in the physical environment? Is it changed by deviations in the social environment? And does an alteration in the social environment affect group behavior? . . .

On the basis of . . . modern-day studies by behavioral scientists we can advance certain hypotheses that can be applied to frontier societies:

1. The "primary" or physical environment did not directly determine such cultural deviations as existed on the frontier, although it laid the basis for such deviations by offering individuals a unique man-land ratio that stimulated an urge for self-advancement.
2. The differing *social* environment of frontier communities fostered the growth of unique folk cultures, based on but distinguishable from those of the successive Easts. This was because:
   a. The diversity of ethnic and social types attracted to pioneer settlements contributed to creating a fluid social order where ethnocentrism was lacking.
   b. Social controls and traditionalism were diminished by isolation and the dispersion of settlement, with a corresponding impetus to innovation.
   c. The absence of a solidified social order with established in-groups and out-groups allowed opportunity for greater vertical mobility.

In essence, then, the principal effect of the frontier social environment was to weaken traditional controls and values. The pioneer found himself in a fluid, ever-changing, unstabilized society, where accustomed behavior did not bring predictable results and where experimentation seemed more essential than in established cultures. Change, not tradition, was the order of life.

Just as important was the fact that the pioneers realized that in moving westward they severed their ties with tradition. The act of migration disrupted the social relationships that had assisted them in patterning their behavior in their old homes. In their new homes the sense of nonbelonging was accentuated, for most frontier communities were settled by men and women from a variety of places and social backgrounds; Yankees and Yorkers, Southerners and Northerners, natives and immigrants, all met and mingled on a common ground. Language barriers and differing social customs made cohesion difficult, for a Vermonter in Illinois might not be able to communicate with the German who lived nearby, or might feel superior to the Tennessee uplander who had taken out the next farm. Distances between neighbors, growing steadily greater as the frontier moved westward across the prairies and plains of mid-America, also heightened the feeling of removal from the group, as did the economic uncertainty of life in an untested new region. The typical frontiersman was oppressed by a sense of social weightlessness (to borrow a term from the space age), which generated a feeling of not belonging fatal to cultural cohesiveness.

The result was a mild form of mass anomie everywhere on the frontier. To some degree all pioneers, even those who succeeded most rapidly, felt a sense of social deprivation, based on their failure to establish comforting social relationships with their neighbors, the absence of defined social norms, and the failure of the new land to meet their unrealistic expectations. This was reflected in the lawlessness and disorder usual in most frontier communities, by the emotional religious practices common there, and by continuing mobility. It was revealed also by the greater degree of political participation in frontier areas as individuals sought to gain status and economic benefits by assuming leadership roles in the unstructured society. These attitudes and desires marked frontier communities as different from those with tightly structured cultures. Rarely had society been so disrupted, so fluid, and so susceptible to forces inviting change. Here was a new social environment, powerful enough to alter men and institutions.

Let no one, however, be misled into believing that the frontier could affect *major* changes in either the personalities or the behavioral patterns of frontiersmen. As in human behavior today, the bulk of the customs and beliefs of the pioneers were transmitted, and were only slightly modified by the changing culture in which they lived. . . .

No *physical* environment could have weakened . . . allegiance to traditionalism, but not even established custom could withstand the corroding impact of the frontier *social* environment. Behavioral patterns, value scales, and modes of thought that emerged in early pioneer communities and that were carried from community to community by successive waves of advancing frontiersmen proved too powerful to be resisted. Even the "ethnic pockets" that clung most doggedly to Old World habits were affected as American neighbors demonstrated the practicality of frontier-tested practices. A German traveler in the West, after noting that one of his newly arrived countrymen looked completely out of place, went on: "Visit him on his thriving farm ten years hence, and, except in the single point of language, you will find him (unless he has settled among a nest of his countrymen) at home among his neighbors, and happily conforming to their usages." Even the most hidebound Englishman learned, as one of them observed, "that he has got to a place where it answers to spend land to save labour, the reverse of his experience in England; and he soon becomes as slovenly a farmer as the American, and begins immediately to grow rich." Conformity to a unique social environment was easier than resistance. The frontier did alter individuals and institutions.

For the spatial frontier, to the visitor or new settler, was a different world. Those who crossed the borderline and recorded their impressions spoke of a cultural fault as observable as a geological fault. Beyond they found a people who behaved and thought and lived in a manner distinctly different from Easterners. Here was "a state of society wholly differing from any that we had seen before," wrote one traveler, and another felt that he was suddenly "a stranger among a people, whose modes of existence and ways of thinking are of a widely different character from those, in the midst of which he has been reared." Americans were as conscious of the division between East and West as travelers from overseas. "Language, ideas, manners, customs—all are new," observed a pioneer newly arrived in backwoods Michigan; "yes, even language; for to the instructed person from one of our great Eastern cities, the talk of the true back-woodsman is scarcely intelligible." Added another from the Ohio Valley frontier of the 1830s: "The people of the west, viewed as individuals, resemble the inhabitants of almost every clime; but taken as a whole, they are unlike every people under heaven. They have come hither from the four quarters of the globe, with manners and habits and genius and temperament, as different as the nations from which they have severally sprung. Every thing is new, just coming into existence." These observers, and others like them, were acutely aware that the social environment of the frontier was distinct from that of the East.

These differences, moreover, were altering the whole national character and converting the Americans into a people strangely unlike the Europeans from whom they sprang. "If I were to draw a comparison between the English and Americans," one English traveler decided, "I should say that there is almost as much difference between the two nations . . . as there has long been between the English and the Dutch"; another judged them to be "as unlike the English as any people can well be." Significantly, the features that most clearly marked the Americans as unique were frontier characteristics, and were found most deeply etched in the West. Travelers observed there the "slight, but perceptible peculiarities of national character which our peculiar circumstances and condition have imposed upon us"; those same traits were "least observable where the population is most mixed, and are scarcely perceptible in our larger commercial towns and cities." Lord Bryce, one of the most penetrating observers of nineteenth-century America, believed that the West was the most distinctively American part of America, precisely because the points in which it differed from the East were the points in which America as a whole differed from Europe. . . .

How accurate were these observations? That question cannot be answered without an understanding of what a "national character" is and is not. A national character is not an absolute quality persisting unchanged through the ages any more than it is a body of characteristics shared by every single person in a country. It rests neither on geographic adjacence nor on a commonly shared historical experience. Above all, national character is not, as was so often stated in the nineteenth century, a product of ethnic grouping mirroring hereditary racial traits. Historians, discouraged by the inaccuracy of these traditional concepts, have been sometimes inclined to deny that a national character has existed. This is unfortunate, for the term is definable and the concept is an essential tool in historical interpretation.

Modern social scientists view national character as a product of both group culture, and "personality." Group culture is the accepted pattern of behavior in any society. "Personality" may be defined as the body of habits, traits, and attitudes of an individual as they are shaped both by his inner motivations and goals, and by his role in the group of which he is a part. Implicit in this definition is the understanding that the group culture partly determines personality, for the individual's goals and motives are influenced by the goals and motivations of the group. A "go-ahead" society such as that of mid-nineteenth century America helps endow its members with the go-ahead spirit. The determinant of national character, then, is the group culture acting upon and molding the personality of individuals. This concept recognizes that the national character changes as the culture changes and is not immutable; similarly, it acknowledges that individuals respond in differing ways to group influences and hence that national character is reflected in various ways among different people. Most important of all, it equates national character with neither race nor physical environment, yet is postulated on the belief that an altered social environment affects the culture, which in turn affects the individual. The personality of the individual and the culture of the group alike respond to changes in the social environment.

The interaction of group culture and personality creates within a nation a body of beliefs and behavior patterns that are widely recognized, both at home and abroad, as being more common there than elsewhere. This "national character" is a historically conditioned and commonly shared system of values and practices. It is, as one social scientist has said, the kind of character that makes the members of a society *want* to act the way they *have* to act as members of that society. Obviously the needs and demands of a society change constantly, and as they do the social organization changes together with the demands for conformity placed upon its members. Hence the "national character" is fluid and changes as the society and culture change. Obviously, too, all individuals within a social group do not develop personalities reflecting the national character. Rebels persist within any society, although their conduct is governed by the rules of that society governing rebels. Yet pressure for conformity is constant; all social groups reward those who follow an accepted behavior pattern and punish those who do not.

In applying these concepts to the United States, the American national character can be defined and its characteristics identified only by separating the basic forces *creating* that shared behavior pattern which is the national character, from the *manifestations* of that character.

Social scientists have isolated four basic elements that help shape the unique attitudes and traits of the people of the United States. One is the motivation that impels Americans; their ambition is success and they measure their worth as much by the upward distance they have traveled in society as by the position they have reached. They think in terms of social mobility and movement along the social ladder rather than of compartmentalized classes or stability; as a result they are excessively concerned with conformity, which seems essential to win the support of their peers needed for each upward move.

Secondly, Americans differ from other peoples in their inner direction. Their ancestors in medieval days were "tradition-directed" as they conformed to the fixed rules of a stabilized society; with the greater freedom possible in modern times, men became increasingly "inner-directed" as they followed individual bents in achieving success. This "inner direction" persisted through the nineteenth century, but in the twentieth a changed economy decreed that most individuals could no longer gain a living simply by mastering an environment; they must win the favor of those about them and shape their conduct to that expected by society. They had become "other-directed," and had replaced their gyroscope with a radar screen. This change from "inner-directed" to "other-directed" is uniquely American, and helps define the national character.

A third key to understanding the people of the United States is the intense competition that serves as a stimulus to their actions. Rivalry is a part of men's lives, and with it a hostile tension that breeds distrust of others. This in turn fosters a sense of failure that stimulates a craving for love and recognition. Americans are unique in their excessive insistence on affection and glorification. Finally, social scientists insist that American culture is unique in its predilection with the individual. In other cultures tradition and the group govern behavior, but in the United States these controls have diminished until the people are oppressed by a sense of social and psychological isolation. This leads to violent exhibits of emotion, expressed especially in manifestations of gladness or sorrow.

Social scientists believe, then, that Americans stand apart because of the strength of their drive toward success and the resulting social mobility, their dependence on the opinions of their contemporaries, their preoccupation with the individual as opposed to the social group, and the inner tensions that result from inevitable failure in a highly competitive society. All of these observations have one thing in common: They stress the competition that governs behavior in the United States. It is this that drives men up the ladder of success, makes them dependent on the favors of their peers, stokes their inner conflicts, and impels them toward an individual-centered existence in which they seek self-elevation without regard to the welfare of society. The American character is, in essence, a group of responses to a highly competitive culture. . . .

One major question must be answered before turning from this portrait of the American character sketched by observers and modern scholars: What was the source of these traits and beliefs? Some students insist that travelers exaggerated the uniqueness of the nation's culture, and that American civilization is only a carbon copy of the British civilization from which it sprang. Those preaching this view hold that migrating Englishmen left behind their feudal institutions, but brought a training in democracy and industrialization that matured rapidly in a land where the retarding influence of traditionalism was lacking. Thus the differences between Britain and the United States are of degree rather than kind, and owe nothing to the physical or social environment of the New World.

Other modern scholars have traced the distinctiveness of American culture to its agrarian background. The extensive agriculture suitable to New World conditions, they argue, forced the farmers who formed the bulk of the population to develop traits now considered uniquely American: the habit of hard work, materialistic attitudes distrustful of cultural achievement, individualism, wastefulness, social and physical mobility. Still other investigators find the key to the national character in the cry of a twentieth century visitor from Russia: "One must remember the age of the country to understand Americans." They maintain that the absence of a feudal past allowed the United States to step into the modern world without the encumbrance of a rigid class structure, outworn economic practices, and traditions that weighed against optimism, social mobility, individualism, and other noticeable American traits. These traits were those of any modern people, appearing first among the Americans but shared by all the Western world eventually.

Two other theories contribute to the total picture. One traces the national character to the abundant natural resources of the New World; as these were utilized over the course of centuries in a series of sequential steps made possible by technological improvements the United States became a "land of plenty" where unparalleled opportunity bred individualism, democracy, mobility, and optimism. The other finds the mobility of the American people their most distinguishing trait, and that this "locomotive instinct" has in turn fathered their social mobility, their democratic practices, their impatience with obstacles to individual self-advancement, and their optimistic belief in a better future. The "M-Factor" in American history, argue the proponents of this theory, was principally important in creating the national character.

Without special pleading, it must be pointed out that all of these explanations stem immediately or remotely from the "frontier hypothesis" of Frederick Jackson Turner. The agricultural practices that left their mark originated precisely because American farmers were pushing into virgin lands instead of following the traditional customs of Europe. The medieval heritage played little part in the nation's development simply because an attractive man-land ratio lured settlers across the seas, forcing them to discard cultural baggage along the way. The New World was a land of plenty solely because its resources were untapped at the time of discovery, and only partially exploited by the early developers. Mobility became a habit largely because Americans contracted the habit of moving as they advanced into unoccupied lands. Once this habit was established their attachment to place lessened; they could move from east to west, from job to job, from city to city, and from country to city. In other words, the relative vacuum of cheap lands that attracted Europeans to America and Americans to the West accounted for the agricultural practices, the newness, the resources, and the physical mobility of the people of the United States. Had the North American continent been settled by an advanced people in 1492, none of these forces could have operated exactly as they have.

Professor of American History at Stanford University since 1961, DAVID POTTER (b. 1910) has had a considerable influence upon American historiography. *People of Plenty,* published in 1954, was written in an attempt to apply the principles and methods of the behavioral sciences to the problems of American history. The present selection re-examines the frontier thesis and argues that the frontier phenomenon was only one form of abundance which shaped American culture and character.*

David Potter

Abundance

. . . [N]o historian can overlook the fact that American history has long provided a classic formula for defining and explaining the American character: this is Frederick Jackson Turner's frontier hypothesis. In any appraisal of what history has to contribute, therefore, it is inevitable that we should return ultimately to the Turner theory. And in any evaluation of the factor of abundance, it is vital to establish what relation, if any, existed between the frontier influence specifically and the general influence of economic abundance. . . .

Turner's paper on "The Significance of the Frontier in American History" was not only a turning point in the development of American historical writing; it was also, in the most explicit sense, an explanation of American character, and might, with perfect validity, have been entitled "The Influence of the Frontier on American Character." Passages throughout the essay may be cited to justify this assertion. For instance, Turner declared that, on the frontier, the "perennial rebirth" of society, the "fluidity of American life, this expansion westward with its new opportunities, it continuous touch with the simplicity of primitive society furnish the forces dominating American character." And, again, "to the frontier, the American intellect owes its striking characteristics." . . .

But, in so far as the frontier hypothesis is related to the factor of abundance, it

*Extracts reprinted from *People of Plenty: Economic Abundance and the American Character* by permission of The University of Chicago Press and David Potter. Published 1954. Eighth impression 1963. Footnotes omitted.

behooves us to take account of it here; and, in fact, it is intimately related. Turner himself said, "the Western wilds, from the Alleghanies to the Pacific, constituted the richest free gift that was ever spread out before civilized man. . . . Never again can such an opportunity come to the sons of men." And, specifically linking this opportunity with the frontier, he added, "The most significant thing about the American frontier is that it lies at the hither edge of free land."

Of course, it should be recognized at once that Turner conceived of other factors besides abundance as being present in the frontier condition. To name only two, there was a temporary lowering of civilized standards, and there was a weakening of the power of traditional institutions such as church and school, with a corresponding enhancement of the stature of the individual.

Therefore we are dealing with abundance as one in a complex of factors, and it becomes important to determine, as far as we can, how much of the influence of what Turner called the "frontier" lay in its being on the outskirts of civilization and how much lay in its function as the locus of maximum access to unused resources. The question is a critical one because, if the factor of abundance was really primary, if the most significant thing about the frontier was, as Turner himself asserted, its contiguity to free land, then we ought to recognize the primacy of abundance and speak of the influence of abundance, in whatever form it occurs, and not restrictively in only one of its manifestations—the frontier manifestation. Do we really mean the influence of the frontier, or do we mean the influence of a factor that was especially conspicuous in the frontier situation but that also operated apart from it upon many other parts of American experience? In so far as the latter is what we mean, we might justifiably regard Turner's famous paper as being, in essence, a study of the significance of economic abundance in American history. . . .

. . . [I]f Turner did not use the term "frontier" to mean various things at various times, at least he used it in a way that placed heavy stress first on one aspect, then on another, with very little notice to the reader that the cluster of ideas back of the term was being substantially changed. No doubt he was right in the view that a whole complex of factors was associated with the westward advance of settlement and that all these factors ought to be taken into account. But his technique, very frustrating to many critics of the last two decades, was instead of treating the separate constituents as separate constituents, to fuse all and discuss them interchangeably under the rubric "frontier." George Wilson Pierson, who has made a careful analysis of this shifting concept, remarks ruefully that, to Turner, "the West was rough (a geographic factor) and it was empty (a sociological force). Perhaps, then, Turner's greatest achievement was his successful marriage of these two dissimilar forces in the single phrase, *free land.*"

The real key, however, to Turner's thought—both in its strength and in its limitations—will never be grasped if we suppose that this elusiveness of definition was simply the result of a vagueness of mind or an indifference to analysis. It is rather, as Henry Nash Smith has recently argued, the result of Turner's personal predilection for one special social ideal—the ideal of agrarian democracy. As Smith expresses this, "from the time of Franklin down to the end of the frontier period almost a century and a half later, the West had been a constant reminder of the importance of agriculture in American society. It had nourished an agrarian philosophy and an agrarian myth that purported to set forth the character and destinies of the nation. The philosophy and the myth affirmed an admirable set of values, but they ceased very early to be useful in interpreting American society as a whole, because they offered no intellectual apparatus for taking account of the industrial revolution. A system which revolved about a half-mystical conception of nature and held up as an ideal a rudimentary type of agriculture was powerless to confront issues arising from the advance of technology. Agrarian theory encouraged men to ignore the industrial revolution altogether, or to regard it as an unfortunate and anomalous violation of the natural order of things. In the . . . sphere of historical scholarship, for example, the agrarian emphasis of the frontier hypothesis has tended to divert attention from the problems created by industrialization for a half-century during which the United States has become the most powerful industrial nation in the world." Turner's "problem"—the one that he set for himself—was "to find a basis for democracy in some aspect of civilization as he observed it about him in the United States. His determined effort in this direction showed that his mind and his standards of social ethics were subtler and broader than the conceptual system within which the frontier hypothesis had been developed, but he was the prisoner of the assumptions he had taken over from the agrarian tradition."

Applying this dictum specifically to the factor of abundance, one can readily verify Smith's general observations. What happened was that, when abundance operated within an agrarian context—in the form of free land for farmers—Turner seized upon it, but with a tendency to identify the factor with the context, to attribute to the context the results that followed from the operation of the factor, while refusing to recognize the operation of the factor when it occurred outside the selected context.

In this connection it would be misleading to say that Turner refused to admit the existence of nonagrarian frontiers. On the contrary, he mentioned them explicitly and specified also that various frontiers offered various conditions and inducements. In his own words, "the unequal rate of advance compels us to distinguish the frontier into the trader's frontier, the rancher's frontier, or the miner's frontier, and the farmer's frontier."

But although these dissimilarities forced him grudgingly—"compelled" him, in his own revealing phrase—to give formal recognition to a variety of frontiers, they conspicuously failed to compel him to broaden his concept of the frontier sufficiently to accomodate them. When he came to such matters as the exploitation of salt, coal, oil, and other mineral resources, he would neither separate them out, thus conceding the limitations of his agrarian hypothesis, nor include them actively in his calculations, thus modifying and qualifying the agrarian tenor of his theme. . . .

Because of these anomalies and because of the presence of concealed agrarian dogma in what purports to be an environmental analysis, it becomes important to consider a little more closely what the elements were in the frontier situation as Turner conceived it. . . .

Most of the things which the frontier meant to Turner are embraced, I believe, by one or another of these factors. It was the place where free land lay at the edge of settlement; the place where institutions no longer towered over the individual man; the place where European complexity gave way to American simplicity; and the place where democratic growth and change was repeatedly reenacted as a process and reaffirmed as a principle. . . .

Such, then, were the main elements of the frontier hypothesis, as Turner developed it: West of the Alleghenies lay a vast expanse of fertile and unsettled land which became available almost free to those who would cultivate it. Across this area, a frontier or edge of settlement pushed steadily west, and along this frontier individuals who had advanced ahead of society's usual institutional controls accepted a lowering of standards at the time for the sake of progress in the future. Constantly repeating over again a democratic experience, they reinforced the national democratic tradition. All these conditions, of course, influenced the mental traits of those who were directly or indirectly involved in the process, and especially their nationalism, their democracy, and this individualism were stimulated. Certain other qualities—a coarseness, combined with a strength, a practicality and materialism of mind, a restless energy, and a measure of buoyancy or exuberance—were all traceable to this frontier influence.

With this outline of the frontier hypothesis in mind, we can now revert to the question: To what extent was the frontier merely the context in which abundance occurred? To what extent does it explain developments which the concept of abundance alone could not explain?

At times Turner himself seemed almost to equate the frontier with abundance, as, for instance, when he said, "These free lands promoted individualism, economic equality, freedom to rise, democracy." It is probably valid to criticize him for this. But if there was a fallacy in his failure to distinguish between these coinciding factors and his consequent practice of treating qualities which were intrinsically derived from abundance as if they were distinctive to the frontier, it would be the same fallacy in reverse to treat qualities which were instrinsically frontier qualities as if they were attributable to abundance. Bearing this caveat in mind, we can hardly deny that there were a number of influences which were peculiar to the frontier or to abundance in its distinctive frontier form and which did not operate outside the frontier phase. For instance, the pioneer's necessity of submitting to hardships and low living standards as the price of higher standards later must certainly have stimulated his optimism and his belief in progress. Similarly, one can hardly doubt that the mingling of peoples on the frontier and their urgent need for federal legislative measures must have stimulated the growth of nationalism just as Turner said. And again, at an even deeper level, it is hard to doubt that the frontier projection of the individual ahead of society and the self-sufficing way of life on the edge of settlement must have greatly stimulated American individualism.

But even to say that Turner was right in all these matters is not to say that he took a comprehensive view of the American experience. By confining his explanation of Americanism to the conditions of the pioneer stage of our development, he placed himself in the position of implying that nothing distinctively American would be left, except as a residue, after the pioneer stage had been passed. By limiting his recognition of abundance to its appearance in the form of free land, he limited his recognition of successive American democratic readjustments to the successive settlement of new areas of free land, and thus he cut himself off from a recognition of the adjustments to technological advance, to urban growth, and to the higher standard of living, all of which have contributed quite as much as the frontier to the fluidity and facility for change in American life. Further, by failing to recognize that the frontier was only one form in which America offered abundance, he cut himself off from an insight into the fact that other forms of abundance had superseded the frontier even before the supply of free land had been exhausted, with the result that it was not really the end of free land but rather the substitution of new forms of economic activity which terminated the frontier phase of our history. . . .

It is now sixty years since Turner wrote his famous essay. For two-thirds of this period his ideas commanded vast influence and indiscriminate acceptance, and then they encountered a barrage of criticism as severe as it was belated. Some aspects of his thought have received such devastating analysis that no historian today would be likely to make the error of adopting them. For instance, historians today would be wary of the agrarian assumptions in Turner's formulation. But the geographical determinism or environmentalism of Turner still possesses great vitality. The strength of its appeal was demonstrated again in 1952 more strikingly, perhaps, than ever before in this country, with the publication by Walter P. Webb of another and a broader restatement of the frontier hypothesis —not for the United States alone, this time, but for the entire planet.

Webb's *Great Frontier* cuts free of both the restrictive Americanism and the restrictive agrarianism of Turner to propose the thesis that the world frontier, opened up by the age of discovery, was "inherently a vast body of wealth without proprietors," that it precipitated a "sudden, continuing, and every-increasing flood of wealth" upon the centers of Western civilization, thus inaugurating a period of boom which lasted about four hundred years and during which all the institutions—economic, political, and social—evolved to meet the needs of a world in boom.

In his explicit recognition that the very essence of the frontier was its supply of unappropriated wealth, Webb has clarified a vital factor which remained obscure in Turner, for Turner seemed to sense the point without clearly stating it, and Turner always neglected forms of wealth other than soil fertility. Webb, with his attention to the precious metals and even more with his focus upon the importance of "that form of wealth classed as Things or commodities," everlastingly breaks the link between agrarian thought and the frontier doctrine. Through his clear perception of the part played by abundance, he has demonstrated in thorough and convincing fashion the validity of the precise point which I have attempted to put forward in this analysis.

If it were only a question whether the frontier has significance intrinsically as a locus of wealth, therefore, my comment would be only to echo Professor Webb; but there is another question: whether the *only* significant source of modern wealth is the frontier. Webb seems to contend that it is, for he asserts that "it was the constant distribution on a nominal or free basis of the royal or public domain that kept the boom going and that gave a peculiar dynamic quality to Western civilization for four centuries," and his discussion is pervaded with dark forebodings for the future of a world which no longer commands such a stock of untapped resources.

The present study has been built, in

large part, upon the theme of American abundance, which is, of course, New World abundance and therefore, in large measure, frontier abundance. This theme is, in many respects, fully in accord with Professor Webb's and at first glance might appear identical with it. But, at the point where Webb attributes to the frontier an exclusive function, my argument diverges from his. . . . I have already sought to show that American abundance has been in part freely supplied by the bounty of nature, but also that it has been in part socially created by an advancing technology, and that neither of these factors can explain modern society without the other. Abundance, as a horse-breeder might say, is by technology out of environment. Professor Webb has treated the subject as if environment bred abundance by spontaneous generation.

To approach the matter more explicitly, let us consider the basis of our present standard of living, which reflects the supply of goods of all kinds. This standard results not merely from our stock of resources, for primitive peoples with bare subsistence standards have possessed the same resources for as long as fifty thousand years. It results also from our ability to convert these resources into socially useful form—that is, from our productive capacity. Our productive capacity, in turn, depends not only on the raw materials, which are ready to hand, but even more upon our ability to increase, through mechanization, the volume of goods which can be turned out by each worker. . . .

If abundance is to be properly understood, it must not be visualized in terms of a storehouse of fixed and universally recognizable assets, reposing on shelves until humanity, by a process of removal, strips all the shelves bare. Rather, abundance resides in a series of physical potentialities, which have never been inventoried at the same value for any two cultures in the past and are not likely to seem of identical worth to different cultures in the future. As recently as twenty years ago, for example, society would not have counted uranium among its important assets. When abundance exercises a function in the history of man, it is not as an absolute factor in nature to which man, as a relative factor, responds. Rather, it is as a physical and cultural factor, involving the interplay between man, himself a geological force, and nature, which holds different meanings for every different human culture and is therefore relative.

In short, abundance is partly a physical and partly a cultural manifestation. For America, from the eighteenth to the twentieth century, the frontier was the focus of abundance, physically because the land there was virgin and culturally because the Anglo-Americans of that time were particularly apt at exploiting the new country. At this lowest threshold of access to abundance, the pioneers found an individualism and a nationalism which they might not have found at other thresholds. But, though physically the frontier remained the site of virgin land, cultural changes gave to the people an aptitude for exploiting new industrial potentialities and thus drew the focus of abundance away from the frontier. But this change of focus itself perpetuated and reinforced the habits of fluidity, of mobility, of change, of the expectation of progress, which have been regarded as distinctive frontier traits. The way in which this happened suggests that it was, in reality, abundance in any form, including the frontier form, rather than the frontier in any unique sense, which wrought some of the major results in the American experience. The frontier remained of primary significance precisely as long as it remained the lowest threshold of access to America's abundance; it ceased to be primary when other thresholds were made lower, and not when the edge of unsettled land ceased to exist. American abundance, by contrast, has remained of primary significance both in the frontier phase and in the vast industrial phase which has dominated American life for the past three-quarters of a century. American development and the American character are too complex to be explained by any single factor, but, among the many factors which do have to be taken into account, it is questionable whether any has exerted a more formative or more pervasive influence than the large measure of economic abundance which has been so constantly in evidence.

An English anthropologist, GEOFFREY GORER (b. 1905) employs psychoanalytic theory in his study, *The American People,* published in 1948. Gorer believes that the rejection of the father is a basic psychological phenomenon which has played a significant historical role in the formation of American national character. He is one of a number of social scientists who have sought to enhance the historical perspective of the problem through evaluation of behavioral factors which enable one to analyze more systematically the process of character formation.*

Geoffrey Gorer

Rejection of Authority

In 1860 the population of the United States, immigrant and native born, white and Negro, young and old, numbered a little over thirty million. In the seventy years that followed, just on thirty million European immigrants crossed the ocean and became Americans. What proportion of the hundred and eighteen million white Americans (the figure of the 1940 census) are descended from ancestors who had arrived before 1860, and what from ancestors who had arrived after, cannot be determined with any exactness; but it is worth recalling that whereas the resident population was composed of all ages, the immigrant population consisted predominantly of young people at the age of greatest fertility.[1]

. . .With few exceptions the immigrants did not cross the ocean as colonists, to reproduce the civilizations of their homes on distant shores; with the geographical separation they were prepared to give up, as far as lay in their power, all their past: their language and the thoughts which only that language could express; the laws and allegiances which they had been brought up to observe; the values and

[1] In 1940 about eleven and a half million white Americans were foreign born and twenty-three million were of foreign-born parents (Statistical Abstracts, 1945).

assured way of life of their ancestors and their former compatriots; even to a large extent their customary ways of eating, of dressing, of living. Most of them escaped at the same time from discriminatory laws, rigidly hierarchical social structures, compulsory military service and authoritarian limitation of the opportunities open to the enterprising and of the goals to which they could aspire. But the rejection of home and country could not be piecemeal; the supports had to be abandoned with the restraints; individually the immigrants had to try to transform themselves into Americans.

Unless they had immigrated as children, or had quite exceptional psychological plasticity, this self-transformation was impossible in its entirety. Culture is strong and pervasive, and the national character which is the embodiment of a local culture is acquired above all in the earlier years of life; will power alone is not enough to modify those motives and ways of viewing the universe which spring from unrecognized and unconscious sources; the majority of mankind cannot remold themselves by taking thought. Consequently the greater number of immigrants, though they had rejected as much of Europe as they could, were still incomplete Americans; their own persons, their characters, their ways of thought, usually their accent, carried the stigmata of the Europe they had rejected. But though they could not transform themselves, their children would be transmuted; the public schools, in some cases aided by the neighbors, would turn their children into the hundred per cent Americans they could never hope to be themselves. And when this transmutation had taken place the parents themselves would be rejected as old-fashioned, ignorant, and in significant ways alien. The more successful the immigrant father was in turning his children into Americans, so that they had no other allegiances or values, the more his foreignness became a source of shame and opprobrium, the less important did he become as a model and guide and exemplar. Whatever her language and ways, the mother retained emotional importance as a source of love and food and succor; but to grow up to be like the father, to do no better than he had done, to be the same sort of person as he was, would be failure indeed and would be so regarded by the father as much as by the son.

It is this break of continuity between the immigrants of the first generation and their children of the second generation which is to my mind of major importance in the development of the modern American character, which gave rise to what might be called, by analogy with genetics, the American mutation. It is true that in nearly all other parts of the world and in many periods individuals have changed their country of allegiance and have seen their children acquire characters and adopt values which were alien to them; but in these other cases the numbers of immigrants were insignificant in proportion to the populations of their host countries, whereas in many areas of the United States, particularly in the cities, they greatly outnumbered the older Americans; in the other cases the rejection of the father as a guide and model was a private solution to a personal problem; in the United States it was also an act which symbolized the acceptance of the dominant values of the society to which they had pledged allegiance. The individual rejection of the European father as a model and a moral authority, which every second-generation American had to perform, was given significance and emphasis by its similarity to the rejection of England by which America became an independent nation.

Modern history offers no easy parallel to the psychological and political conditions which accompanied the separation of the American colonies from England in the second half of the eighteenth century. Until a bare thirteen years before the Declaration of Independence and the outbreak of war the allegiance of the colonists to England seems to have been unquestioned. In local matters they were mostly self-governing, but they considered themselves loyal subjects of the king of England, on a par with his subjects everywhere. Their outlook, their institutions, their philosophy and their religion all stemmed from England; the variations from the norm were no greater than those between one English region and another; the impact of novel foreign ideas (in particular French) was not greater in America than in London.

Between 1763 and 1776 this allegiance was destroyed for a significant number of the colonists by a series of arbitrary and high-handed acts on the part of George III and some of his ministers, which placed the colonists in an inferior position compared with the other subjects of the king, in that taxes were levied on them, troops quartered on them, and their commerce interfered with, without their consent. These departures from English practice were resisted in the name of English principles; when the recognized legal methods of obtaining redress were rendered fruitless by the blind obstinacy of the king and his ministers, the colonists, still acting on English precedent, took to arms to defend "the rights of Englishmen."

In the course of a protracted and often desperate war the allegiance to England was thrown off by the greater number of the colonists, including the most influential. This throwing off of the English allegiance was the rejection of the only embodied authority which was generally recognized; it was not, in those years, the replacement of one authority by another. The birth of the American republic was signalized by the rejection of authority as such: authority was coercive, arbitrary, despotic, morally wrong.

For eleven years the thirteen independent colonies pursued often mutually contradictory policies, linked only in a powerless voluntary confederation; but the almost complete bankruptcy to which this near anarchy brought the Confederation showed that it was impossible for them to survive without some sort of central authority; and in 1787 a Constitutional Convention was held to devise a federal government which would have the minimum of authority necessary for the independent survival of the United States. The remarkable document which was the outcome of these deliberations—the American Constitution—is especially noteworthy for the ingenuity with which authority is jealously circumscribed; the system of checks and balances and the principle of divided powers were intended to erect insuperable legal barriers to the excessive authority of one person or group.

In some significant ways the birth of the American republic can be compared with the mythological scene which Freud imagined for the origin of civilization and the institution of totemic observances. In Freud's "Just So" story the downtrodden sons combine together to kill the tyrannical father; then, overwhelmed by their crime, and fearful that one of their number will attempt to take the murdered father's place, they make a compact which establishes the legal equality of the brothers, based on the common renunciation of the father's authority and privileges. England, the England of George III and Lord North, takes the place of the despotic and tyrannical father, the American colonists that of the conspiring sons, and the Declaration of Independence and the American Constitution that of the compact by which all Americans are guaranteed freedom and equality on the basis of the common renunciation of all authority over people, which had been the father's most hated and most envied privilege.

This is of course only an analogy derived from a parable, but it does symbolize a number of major psychological truths. From the emergence of America as an independent nation two major themes appear as characteristic of Americans: the emotional egalitarianism which maintains that all (white American) men are equal to the extent that the subordination of one man to another is repugant and legally forbidden, equal in opportunity and legal position; and the belief that authority over people is morally detestable and should be resisted, that the suspicion that others are seeking authority cannot be too vigilant, and that those who occupy the necessary positions of authority within the state should be considered as potential enemies and usurpers. The prized equality of Americans was and is dependent on the weakness of their government.

As the immigrants' children learned to become one hundred per cent Americans in school, these lessons were impressed upon them continuously in their classrooms, in their lessons and textbooks in history and civics, in the sermons and celebrations which mark the patriotic cycle of holidays. For these children of Europeans the England of the textbooks became a monster of oppression and tyranny, and the throwing off of the English allegiance was stripped of nearly all the ambivalence which had accompanied the historical act; to reject authority became a praiseworthy and specifically American act, and the sanctions of society were added to the individual motives for rejecting the family authority personified in the father; and the father, with his European character and upbringing, was often excessive in his demands for obedience. But whether the individual father hindered or helped his children to become a different sort of person from what he was, was a question of minor importance; the making of an American demanded that the father should be rejected both as a model and as a source of authority. Father never knew best. And once the mutation was established, it was maintained; no matter how many generations separate an American from his immigrant ancestors, he rejects his father as authority and exemplar, and expects his sons to reject him.

Psychoanalytic theory was developed in Europe; and, with the prevalent European social and family structure, it seemed reasonable to maintain that the positions of authority in the state—king, priest, policeman, officer, and so on—were symbolic extensions of the authority of the father. But this statement was based on the unjustified assumption that family forms and the role of the parents were identical everwhere, that all fathers everywhere were awe-inspiring figures of authority. A more valid generalization would be that in any given society at a given time the patterns of authority in different situations tend to resemble one another, that in different contexts the emotional concomitants of superordination and subordination remain similar and interact on one another; the father models his behavior on that of the examples of authority in his society in much the same way that the child interprets social representatives of authority in the light of his attitude toward his father. When an American becomes a father he inevitably tends to maintain his role in a fashion congruent with the values of his society; his biological superiority to the newborn child is adapted to the patterns society gives for proper behavior in positions of superiority.

The typical American attitudes toward authority have remained substantially the same as those manifested by the framers of the American Constitution: authority is inherently bad and dangerous; the survival and growth of the state make it inevitable that some individuals must be endowed with authority; but this authority must be as circumscribed and limited as legal ingenuity can devise; and the holders of these positions should be under constant scrutiny, should be watched as potential enemies.

These attitudes toward the concept of authority over people and toward persons placed in positions of authority are basic to the understanding of American character and American behavior. They are far more than political; they are therefore quite different from the situations in, say, Ireland or Greece where to be "agin the government" is a recognized and respected political position, but where the authority of the church in the one case, and that of the family in the other, generally remains unquestioned. With the rarest exceptions, these attitudes do not involve the abstract idealism of the philosophical anarchism of Spain or nineteenth-century Russia; despite the political implications, they are above all moral: people, or institutions, who "push other people around" are bad, repugnant to decent feelings, thoroughly reprehensible. Authority over people is looked on as a sin, and those who seek authority as sinners.

The implications of these attitudes are manifold, and reach into nearly every sphere of American life. . . .

During all his formative years the young American has continually impressed upon him the proper attitude toward authority, and toward men who try to exercise it. Consequently, when he in his turn becomes a father, he finds his proper role toward his children defined and limited by the negative sanctions against the exercise of authority by one man over another. Even if his temperament made him tend toward dominating his children and exacting unquestioning obedience from them, he would get no support from his wife, his neighbors, or his community. To a certain extent the pattern of authority in the state is reproduced in the family: it is as if the father represented the Executive, the mother the Legislative, and the neighbors, headed by the schoolteacher, the Judiciary authority. The child is in the position of the public, playing off one authority against another, invoking the system of checks and balances to maintain his independence. Although this is a somewhat far-fetched comparison, it more nearly represents the structure of the ordinary American family than does the patriarchal picture derived from Europe, or the mirror image of that picture, with the father's authority transferred wholesale and unaltered to the mother.

The picture of the actual structure of the American family is further confused by the English or European origin of many of the social forms, of much of the law, and some of the religion of the United States. With the exception of the very poorest Negroes, the form of the family is still patriarchal; children still take their father's surname, though the use of the mother's maiden name as a middle name is increasingly common; women have only recently gained full civil and legal equality, and most of the conspicuously honorific positions are still reserved for men. But although the forms are similar, the content is very different from the patriarchal societies of most of Europe and Asia.

The crucial experience of the second generation when the son was transformed into something the father could never be dominates the relations and expectations between all American fathers and their sons. Even if he is not an incomplete American, the father is almost by definition old-fashioned, unaware of the latest fads and fashions which occupy his children, ill at ease among the newly popularized gadgets with which they disport themselves. He is not, or at least not for long, a source of knowledge greater than his children can possess. Like the immigrant father, he does not expect his sons to be like him, to have the same sort of profession or stay in the same social class. His pride and justification depend on his sons' surpassing him and leaving him behind. Except for his fundamental maleness, the father is not a model on which the son is expected to mold himself.

Professor of American History at the State University of New York at Albany since 1965, ARTHUR A. EKIRCH, JR. (b. 1915) has written primarily in the area of intellectual history. His early study, *The Idea of Progress in America: 1815–1860* (1944) traces the European intellectual origins of the Idea of Progress and shows its outworking in American life and thought. Ekirch argues that progress became, in America, a "dogma of widespread mass appeal." It became an underlying dynamic force which contributed significantly to the shaping of American life and character.*

Arthur A. Ekirch, Jr.

The Idea of Progress

Through the course of its long and important history the idea of progress has been defined and interpreted in various ways. This idea that "civilization has moved, is moving, and will move in a desirable direction" has been compared with the concepts of Fate, Providence, or personal immortality. Like those ideas it is believed in not because it is held to be good or bad, nor because it it considered to be true or false. In the words of J. B. Bury, the leading historian of the concept of progress, "belief in it is an act of faith." Bury accordingly included progress among those ideas not dependent for their fulfillment upon man's will. And in this opinion he was supported by many of the European philosophers of the concept. However, in the United States, as we shall see, the American people felt that, although progress was indeed certain, it could nevertheless be impeded or accelerated by human will and effort. It was, therefore, not only a theory of the past or a prophecy of the future, but also an incentive to action. In other words, progress represented a measurable growth in the pursuit of knowledge and in the achievements of science as well as an advance in the ability of men to control for good their own lives and destinies. . . .

The idea enjoyed . . . a position in the intellectual heritage of the world long before the birth of the United States. An important factor in the philosophy and ideology of Western Europe, it was also

*From Arthur A. Ekirch, Jr. *The Idea of Progress in America, 1815–1860* (New York: Columbia University Press, 1944), pp. 11–37. Footnotes omitted.

carried across the Atlantic to the New World, where it prospered in a rich and fertile environment. In America the successful development of a seemingly limitless expanse of land and resources made the people peculiarly susceptible to a belief in so dynamic an idea as that of progress. While their concept of the idea may rightly be considered a part of the European culture pattern transmitted to and modified by the New World, the impact of the American environment made it inevitable that the American people should interpret the idea of progress in the light of their own interests and experience. . . .

The philosophies of progress developed by . . . European thinkers were, of course, known in America. Their treatises were found in the libraries of American intellectuals, and many of the volumes were republished in the United States. Americans went abroad and returned home bringing back their gleanings of European culture. Europeans came to the New World as visitors, settlers, and propagandists. However, the problem of gauging the European influence on the American concept of progress in our period is a part of the general problem of the transfer of ideas and culture between Europe and America. Since this is a subject in need of much further research, only an indication can be given regarding the influence of European thought upon the American idea of progress.

The American theory of progress in the early years of the Republic may be considered a product of the philosophy of the eighteenth-century enlightenment transplanted to the virgin soil of a new nation. During their lives many of the American people had seen the thirteen colonies enjoy a tremendous expansion in population, wealth, and territory. Their own dynamic role in pushing forward the frontier of settlement and in achieving independence from England made such a concept as that of progress congenial to their tastes and experience. In contrast to the "worn-out, effete" monarchies of Europe, it was felt that in the United States the advantages of youth were combined with a superior form of republican government. With a continent opened to the enterprise of its citizens, the faith of a Condorcet or of a Godwin in the powers of science and of human reason to effect progress, was shared by the American philosophers in the first decades of the Republic.

Benjamin Franklin, during the years of his long life from 1706 to 1790, had witnessed many progressive changes in American society. Equally at home on both sides of the ocean, Franklin in the last years of his life related his hopes of future world progress to the advance of science and to the growth of the American political experiment. . . . When the United States itself was undergoing the transformation in its form of government which culminated in the adoption of the Constitution, Franklin in a letter of 1786 to Jonathan Shipley of England wrote:

> You seem desirous of knowing what Progress we make here in improving our Governments. We are, I think, in the right Road of Improvement, for we are making Experiments. I do not oppose all that seem wrong, for the Multitude are more effectually set right by Experience, than kept from going wrong by Reasoning with them. And I think we are daily more and more enlightened; so that I have no doubt of our obtaining in a few Years as much public Felicity, as good government is capable of affording.

During those years around the turn of the century in 1800 Franklin's faith in the progress of the United States was exemplified by a group of patriotic orators and poets who saw in America a land of progress, freedom, and destiny. In the words of a typical Fourth of July orator: "The sun of the old world is setting; of the new just beginning to rise." The same optimistic confidence in the future of the New World was voiced by the poet of the American Revolution, Philip Freneau, and by his fellow American bard, Joel Barlow, who was the more explicit in his exposition of progress. A student at Yale and a chaplain in the American army during the Revolutionary period, Barlow began, soon after the conclusion of that struggle, to write an American epic on the theme of the grand accomplishment of Columbus. In his poem he represented the consequence of Columbus' discovery in the form of a vision in which the great explorer was soothed by the knowledge that his work had not been in vain. Barlow throughout his poem professed a strong faith in progress as the design of Providence. From the advances already made in the arts and sciences by the United States, and with the return of peace, he predicted an enormous worldwide melioration in the future. In the words of the seraph of the vision, addressing Columbus:

> See, thro' the whole, the same progressive plan,
> That draws for mutual succour, man to man,
> From friends to tribes, from tribes to realms ascend,
> Their powers, their interests and their passions blend;
>
> Till tribes and states and empires find their place,
> And one wide interest sways the peaceful race.

A conservative in his youth, Barlow was one of the famous group of Connecticut Federalist poets, the Hartford Wits. However, he later forsook much of his early Puritan and Federalist background in his enthusiasm for the democratic spirit of the age. In 1788 he left America for what was to be a seventeen-year stay in Europe. Happy in his new surroundings, Barlow in *Two Letters to the Citizens of the United States . . . Written from Paris in the Year 1799* expressed the faith in progress typical of the early French Revolutionary philosophy. After stressing the isolation of America and its vast expanse of vacant lands—the guarantee of its character as an agricultural nation—he announced that he looked forward to a future in which science, education, and democracy would unite to create a nation in which peace and progress would rule. Then in 1807 he expanded his *Vision of Columbus* with the publication of a long epic poem, *The Columbiad.* This latter poem furnished an added illustration of the transformation effected by Barlow's experience in France. For his older faith in the Divine will of God as the motivating cause of human progress, Barlow now substituted his enthusiastic belief in the power of science and of human reason. In the Preface he declared that his object was to encourage a love of liberty, peace, and republican principles. Admitting that he could not "expect that every reader, nor even every republican reader, will join me in opinion with respect to the future progress of society and the civilization of states," he, however, stated that "there are two sentiments in which I think all men will agree: that the event is desirable, and that to believe it practicable is one step towards rendering it so."

Barlow in his writings was influenced by the ideas of his friend Thomas Paine, an enthusiastic disciple of the principles of the French Revolution. Characteristic of the Revolution for a time at least was the idea of a progressive crusade destined to culminate in the perfectibility of man and in the confederation of all nations. In the United States Paine, the pamphleteer of the American Revolution, hailed the French struggle as an example of the spread of American principles. Writing in 1791 in reply to Edmund Burke's attack on the French Revolution, Paine emphasized the fact that in a world of change "the opinions of men change also." Opposed to the idea that the future was bound to the prejudices of the past, he rejoiced that "The opinions of men with respect to government are changing fast in all countries. The revolutions of America and France have thrown a beam of light over the world, which reaches into man." In contrast to the wasteful cost of the English monarchy, Paine wrote:

> I see in America the generality of people living in a style of plenty unknown in monarchical countries; and I see that the principle of its government, which is that of the *equal Rights of Man,* is making a rapid progress in the world. . . .
>
> From the rapid progress which America makes in every species of improvement, it is rational to conclude that, if the governments of Asia, Africa and Europe had begun on a principle similar to that of America, or had not been very early corrupted therefrom, those countries must by this time have been in a far superior condition to what they are.

The enthusiasm of Thomas Paine for the principles of the French Revolution was not shared by the conservative Federalist elements in the United States. And with the transformation of the early idealism and radicalism of the Revolution into the conquering nationalism of Napoleon, liberals were also forced to turn from France in their hopes for future world progress. Some indication of the further effect of the French Revolution on the American concept of progress may be discovered in the correspondence on the subject maintained by John Adams and Thomas Jefferson after the close of their active political careers. John Adams, the Federalist and conservative, was a staunch opponent from its inception of the philosophy and actions of the French Revolutionary movement. Familiar with the writings of Condorcet, Adams took pains to deprecate both his originality and greatness. Believing that Europe was toward the close of the eighteenth century "advancing by slow but sure steps towards an amelioration of the condition of man in religion and government, in liberty, equality, fraternity, knowledge, civilization, and humanity," Adams in a letter of 1813 to Jefferson went on to say: "The French Revolution I dreaded, because I was sure it would not only arrest the progress of improvement, but give it a retrograde course, for at least a century, if not many centuries." Skeptical of the extravagant optimism of the early nineteenth century and doubtful that the science of government had yet made much advance, Adams nevertheless on the whole retained his early faith in the progress of science and in the future of America.

The political opponent of Adams on almost all public questions, Thomas Jefferson combined an international outlook with a liberal faith that the United States would be the theatre of the world's future progress. Jefferson did not become discouraged by the periodic retrograde motions which seemed to occur at times like the Napoleonic period, but in 1816, in a letter to John Adams, he predicted:

> We are destined to be a barrier against the returns of ignorance and barbarism. Old Europe will have to lean on our shoulders, and to hobble along by our side, under the monkish trammels of priests and kings, as she can. What a colossus shall we be, when the southern continent comes up to our mark! What a stand will it secure as a ralliance for the reason and freedom of the globe! I like the dreams of the future better than the history of the past.

. . . The faith in progress of the founding fathers like Franklin and Jefferson not only continued to prevail in the period of our survey, but it also became a dogma of widespread mass appeal. With the fall of Napoleon and with the close of the War of 1812 in America, the people of the United States were once more free to pursue the development of their own continent. "In 1815 for the first time Americans ceased to doubt the path they were to follow. Not only was the unity of their nation established, but its probable divergence from older societies was also well defined." While Europe seemed to be fastened in the grip of a political and economic reaction, American independence was now assured. Although the return of peace was followed by a depression lasting until 1820, there was no lack of confidence in the eventual prosperity of the nation. That democracy would grow with the physical expansion of the country seemed also certain. The year 1815 therefore marked the beginning of a period in American history in which new forces of great significance to the idea of progress were unleashed.

However, in spite of the generally favorable conditions prevailing in the United States of 1815 for the growth in popularity of the idea of progress, certain exceptions may be noted. Some of the old Federalists and their descendants still took a pessimistic view of the democratic tendencies which had been growing since the time of Jefferson's capture of the presidency. Also foremost among groups hostile to the idea of radical or inevitable improvement were some of the leading church sects in America. Calvinism remained with its low view of human nature and its adherence to the idea of predestination. The vogue of revivalism and the growth of evangelistic sects meant in part an emphasis on life in the world to come and culminated during the early 1840's in the Millerite's gospel of the approaching end of the world. Throughout the period Catholicism received from among the immigrants many adherents to its authoritarian and generally backward-looking ideology and to its otherworldly outlook. This spread of Catholicism also strengthened the conviction of the nativists that the immigrants were a menace to American progress. Among the poorer classes of farmers and workers the occasional depressions fostered in some measure the feeling that progress was not automatic or inevitable. Intellectuals and reformers, distressed by the ruthless materialism of so much of American progress, sometimes withdrew into an attitude of hopeless pessimism. In the South the necessity of defending slavery imparted in many quarters a generally conservative, backward-looking philosophy of life opposed to the concept of progress entertained in the other parts of the nation. These influences on American thought were, to be sure, not the major note, but they interposed a conservative interpretation which had its effects in modifying the idea of progress.

More positive and dynamic in their influence upon the idea were those aspects of the American scene which gave reality to American optimism in the period from the close of the War of 1812 to the outbreak of the Civil War. In the United States during these decades the material environment and intellectual atmosphere were alike favorable to a philosophy of progress. The ever-expanding frontier and the abundant resources of the youthful nation provided for a rapidly increasing population. Growing from some eight million people in 1815 to over thirty million in 1860, the generous natural increase was augmented by a rising tide of migration from Europe. The comparatively modest numbers of immigrants arriving at first were increased during the latter part of the 1840's. Then during the 1850's the new arrivals, especially from Ireland and Germany, came at an average annual rate of over a quarter of a million.

It was also during these decades that the industrial revolution took strong root and began to flourish in America. In New England cotton manufacturing vied with foreign trade for the dominant position, and in the South the promise of the cotton gin was realized in the processing and marketing of larger crops. These were the decades in which the first railroads were built. In 1844 the telegraph was perfected, and like the canals and railways, it helped to bring the various parts of the country closer together. Throughout the period a vast area of Western lands was also available to settlement, and as the people moved west from the seaboard, immigrants came from Europe to fill their places or go west at their side. Except for the long depression beginning in 1837 and some minor economic crises, the period was one of general prosperity. Since all did not share equally in this material prosperity, the period was also one of growing class and sectional conflicts with the protests against the evils of the rising industrial system exemplified in the numerous reform movements of the day. . . .

Culturally the period also witnessed a great advance. The public school system, under state control and leadership, was established in response to the demands of working men, humanitarian reformers and philanthropists. Helping to fulfill the ideal of an educated population, the lyceum spread "culture" to the interested audiences. Magazines and newspapers grew in numbers and in popularity. The colleges became less exclusive, and some at least came to be more free of religious domination. In keeping with these material evidences of culture a national literature and a national art were developed during the period.

The reality provided by this material and cultural advance also served to strengthen the old idea that America enjoyed an especial and unique position in the world. The American people, imbued with a strong faith in the efficacy of their own physical and intellectual achievements, universalized their experience into a general theory of progress to which the rest of the world was expected to accede. In the eyes of the Americans the older civilization of Europe was already in a state of decay. Confident of their own future in the "era of good feeling" and of youthful nationalism prevailing after 1815, they emphasized the difference between the Old and the New World with the proclamation of the Monroe Doctrine in 1823. Later during the forties and fifties the concept of a peculiar American mission, under the slogans of manifest destiny and of Young America, became transformed into a rationalization for territorial expansion in those regions considered necessary for the westward movement of the Republic. But in its more idealistic aspects the concept of a unique American destiny embraced the hope that democracy, through the force of its peaceful example, might become the form of government for the world. And in religious circles this same faith was related to the spread of Christianity under American auspices. The belief in American institutions, in conjunction with the prosperity of its society, fostered a sentiment of nationalism which was only temporarily interrupted by the Civil War. It also helped to provide the proper material and intellectual setting for the mass reception of the idea of progress. With the concrete evidences of material advancement on every side, progress was the faith of the common man as well as of the philosopher. Sometimes considered as an inevitable law of destiny or of Providence, it was also regarded as an aspiration to be attained by human will and effort.

During the period of our survey the formal definitions of progress embraced the traditional concept of advance and melioration. In contrast to a violent or revolutionary change, progress was considered to involve a regular and gradual process of growth. The concept of intellectual and moral improvement was used to distinguish the idea from those mere material and physical advances which might involve a change without true individual and social betterment. As defined in Europe by generations of intellectuals, it came to be treated as a purely philosophical idea. However, in America the unique experience and concrete achievements of the people helped to give the concept a dynamic reality. No longer only a philosophical theory, but also a demonstrable fact, the idea in the United States of the Middle Period was delivered from the cloister of the scholar into the hands of the people. We shall see, moreover, that the idea of progress was sufficiently vague in its meaning and congenial in its portent to be susceptible of use in justifying even contradictory tendencies in the age of which it was a dominant, if not the most widely cherished, idea.

OSCAR HANDLIN (b. 1915), Professor of History at Harvard University since 1954, established his reputation through his studies of American immigration patterns. His monograph, *Boston's Immigrants* (1941), was followed by the Pulitzer Prize-winning *The Uprooted* (1951) and the broader *Immigration as a Factor in American History* (1959). In *The Americans* (1963) from which this selection is taken, Handlin argues that the American character was shaped in part by a situation which required seekers who wished to achieve security and stability nevertheless to seek out risks in search of reward and plenty.*

Oscar Handlin

The Taking of Risks

Independence marked the political separation of the United States from Europe. But another kind of separation had already been effected by the time that the new state took form. The Americans had become a distinct people. The widening gulf that prevented the colonists and the English ministers from understanding one another was the result of a fundamental divergence of experience. The men on the western shore of the Atlantic had ceased to be the same as those on its older, eastern, shore. In the hearts and minds of those who fought it, therefore, the Revolution was already consummated before the first shot was fired. Even had political developments taken some other turn that permitted the colonies to remain within the empire, the Americans would still have been a nation apart.

The signs of distinctiveness appeared in the middle of the eighteenth century. Earlier, writers who referred to the Americans had in mind the Indian native of the soil. Now the term came consistently to apply to the provincials, as if they were no longer Englishmen living abroad but a separate species. The British officers and men who served in the New World in the wars against France habitually differentiated themselves from the colonists. The Americans did the same. The encounters of travelers—whether the provincials were abroad or the Europeans in the colonies—elicited the same sense of distinctiveness. On the eve of the Revo-

*From *The Americans* by Oscar Handlin, by permission of Atlantic, Little, Brown and Co. and Hutchinson Publishing Group, Ltd., pp. 148–157.

lution, it was clear that a new nationality held together the people of the New World.

Neither then nor later could Americans explain the bonds that held them together as the products of inheritance. The Frenchman or German or Englishman was what he was by virtue of his patrimony; his ancestors had passed down to him a territory, a language, customs and religion which cemented individuals into a unity. Not so the American. His language, laws and customs were mostly English; but that heritage did not establish an identity with the people of the mother country. That was already evident on the eve of the Revolution and the events of the years after 1774 strengthened the convictions that this nation was not simply the derivative offshoot of any other. Heatedly Americans insisted that their English inheritance was only one, if the largest, of several. They were a mixture of many varieties of Europeans who by the alchemy of the New World were fused into a new kind of man.

What then was this new man—the American? Several questions lay hidden in the inquiry. Why did Americans think they were different from other people? Were they actually different? And what made them identify themselves as one nation—rather than as several, as their separate provincial experiences might have forecast. The answers were embedded in the institutions the colonies had developed, in their character as people, and in their aspirations for the future.

Shortly before his death in 1753, William Douglass, a Boston physician, commented on the problem in his *Summary View* of the history and present condition of the British colonies in North America. Douglass had observed that a difference in their experience had set the Americans apart from other Englishmen. Life in the wilderness, the effects of constant mobility, and the necessity of adjusting to strange conditions had nurtured among them novel customs and manners and had created new social forms. He initiated thus a long line of speculation that attributed the nationality of the Americans to their distinctive institutions.

Certainly these factors were important. By the middle of the eighteenth century a variety of circumstances made the culture of the colonies American, in the sense that it was both intercolonial and different from that of England. The provinces were all contiguous, so that men and goods moved freely among them. Ties of trade drew them together; stagecoaches, inns, and a regular post facilitated communications, as did the numerous vessels that plied the coastal sea. Newspapers passed from town to town and made the dispersed population familiar with a common fund of information and ideas. Despite local variations, all the governments were unmarked by significant feudal elements, and notable similarities in style of life knit the several colonies together.

In addition, a common enemy pressed the Americans toward unity. At first it was the French, who for a century were a continuing danger to the frontier. After 1763, when that peril abated, the threat came from the mother country; and the necessity of joining forces in the struggle developed a consciousness of common interest. As the crisis unfolded and as men thought of their differences with England, they became increasingly aware of the similarities among themselves. In 1765 at the Stamp Act Congress, Christopher Gadsden had already proclaimed that *there ought to be no New England man, no New Yorker, known on the Continent; but all Americans.* And ten years later, Patrick Henry had boldly affirmed, *I am not a Virginian but an American.*

The War for Independence was itself a unifying experience and after the peace the recollection of shared sufferings held the victors together. The new governments had many features in common and their emphasis upon free institutions added strength to the sentiment of nationalism. History had thus created a network of common institutions that endowed Americans with nationality.

But here was a paradox! One could speak of American institutions; but for a long time there was no America, except insofar as the term vaguely applied to the whole hemisphere. That designation could be attached to no political entity in existence before 1774. Each colony was separate and related not to its neighbors but to the Crown. Boston's governmental, cultural and business contacts were at least as close with London as with Charleston, South Carolina. Efforts to devise schemes for intercolonial co-operation among the governments were futile; and when the provinces met together it was in congresses, as if they were separate states.

Furthermore, not all the English possessions were American in the sense that they joined the rebellion and became states in the Union. Nova Scotia, Quebec and the West Indian islands remained apart, yet they shared some experiences and institutions with those that became independent. South Carolina, in climate, history and economy, was closer to Barbados than to Massachusetts.

Indeed, diversities were as striking as uniformities in the cluster of mainland colonies that formed the nation. Differences in antecedents, history, habits, religious affiliations, and style of life set the New Englander off from the Virginian, the New Yorker from the Pennsylvanian. Nor did those people learn to discount the differences simply by common exposure to the wilderness. In many respects the diversities remained significant; and, in any case, the towns distant from the frontier were as American as the backcountry.

Remoteness from the Old World was no criterion at all of the degree of national identification. The Americans were by no means those who were un-European; indeed ties across the Atlantic had never been closer than in the quarter-century before Independence. No colonist seemed more representative of his countrymen than Benjamin Franklin and none was more familiar than he in the cosmopolitan salons of Paris.

And who most eloquently expressed the aspirations of the nation as it approached the test of revolution? The Americans commonly agreed that two works, *Letters from an American Farmer* and *Common Sense,* most carefully described them as a people, most accurately enunciated their ideas and attitudes. Yet Michel de Crèvecoeur, the author of the one, was a Frenchman who had only migrated from Canada after 1763; and Thomas Paine had come off the ship from England little more than a year before he wrote the other. Neither could have been shaped by the influence of distinctive institutions or experience in the brief period after his arrival.

There was no America before 1774. But there were Americans. The people of Maine and Georgia did feel a sense of identification with the nation and did regard their institutions and experience as common unifying forces. The circumstances of their lives in the New World alone were not enough to create a national sentiment; but the people, under those circumstances, developed traits of character that drew them together in pursuit of common goals.

That was Crèvecoeur's conclusion when he attempted to account for the identity of his adopted countrymen. He too had puzzled over the question of who the Americans were. He could see clearly enough that they were a mixture of English, Scotch, Irish, French, Dutch, Germans, and Swedes. From this promiscuous breed that race, now called Americans, had arisen. *He was an American, who, leaving behind him all his ancient prejudices and manners, received new ones, from the new mode of life he embraced, the new government he obeyed, the new rank he held.* But, by what invisible power had this surprising metamorphosis been performed? In part, by that of the laws and of a new social system. But whence proceeded these laws? From the government. Whence the government?

There was the difficulty. The colonies were, after all, English; and although the original genius and the strong desire of the settlers influenced the laws, in the last analysis it was the Crown that ratified and confirmed them. Furthermore, these institutions were neither uniform through the many provinces of British America nor entirely distinctive of them. Crèvecoeur pointed to the significant differences between men who lived in the North and those who lived in the South, between those who earned their livelihood by the sea and those who tilled the soil, between the residents of the frontier and the German Moravians.

It was therefore necessary to look not merely at the laws, but at the mode of living in a new society which shaped the character of the people. To do so Crèvecoeur narrowed the focus of his vision from the continent as a whole to a tiny corner of it—the island of Nantucket. Here a society of five thousand individuals exemplified the traits distinctive of the Americans.

Crèvecoeur reviewed at length the topography of the place, the manners of the inhabitants, the way in which they earned their bread, the upbringing of their children and the form of their government. He then passed to a description of the whale fishery, which had begun as the simple pursuit of offshore strays but which now carried the Nantucketers far from home, northward by the coast of Labrador to Cape Desolation and southward by Brazil to the Falkland Islands and even to the South Seas.

In one of these characteristic ventures, a little company forms and sets out in a brig of about 150 tons burden. They have no wages; each draws a certain established share in partnership so that all are equally vigorous and determined. They sail for weeks in readiness for the moment of their great encounter. When they sight the whale, two boats are launched, each with a crew of six, four at the oars, one on his feet in the bow holding a harpoon, and the other at the helm. At a reasonable distance, one boat stands off as a witness, the other approaches.

The harpooner is still; *on him principally depends the success of the enterprise. In his hands he holds the dreadful weapon—made of the best steel, to the shaft of which the end of a cord is firmly tied. The other end is fastened to the bottom of the boat. They row in profound silence, leaving the whole conduct of the contest to the harpooner and to the steersman. At a distance of about fifteen feet, the harpooner bids them stop.*

He balances high his harpoon, trying at this important moment to collect all the energy of which he is capable. He launch-

es it forth—the whale is struck! Sometimes, in the immediate impulse of rage, she will attack the boat and demolish it with one stroke of her tail. At other times she will dive and disappear from sight or swim away and draw the cord with such swiftness that it will set the edge of the boat on fire by the friction. The boat follows her course until, tired at last with convulsing the elements, she dies and floats on the surface.

The handful of men, venturing freely forth to impose their will upon the natural power of sea and whale, are American in character. Why?

The Nantucketers are not alone in the pursuit of the great whale; in the eighteenth century, vessels from England and Scandinavia also expose themselves to the danger. But the motive that leads Nantucketers to the sea marks them off from other seafaring men. Neither failure at home nor despair sends them to that element; it is a simple plan of life, a well-founded hope of earning a livelihood. The sea becomes to them a kind of patrimony; they go to whaling with as much pleasure and tranquil indifference, with as strong an expectation of success, as the landsman undertakes to clear a piece of swamp.

And they go to come back home. Not for them the wild bouts of carousing in port, by which other seamen punctuate their repeated encounters with danger. There are no material irregularities when the fleet returns to Nantucket. All is peace and a general decency prevails. The long abstemiousness to which these men are exposed, the frequent repetitions of danger, the boldness in surmounting them, do not lead, when on shore, to a desire for inebriation and a more eager pursuit of those pleasures of which they have been so long deprived and which they must soon again forego. They come home to their wives and children; and the pleasures of returning to their families absorb every other desire. In their absence, their wives have managed their farms and transacted their business. The men at their return, weary with the fatigue of the sea, full of confidence and love, carefully give their consent to every transaction that has happened during their absence, and all is joy and peace. "Wife, thee hast done well," is the general approbation for application and industry.

The Nantucketers were distinctive not in their willingness to take risks or in the fact that they had homes to which to return, but in the unique juncture of the two qualities. They were stable men who cherished ties to family and friends, who left home not because there was no place, but voluntarily and with the intention of returning. The hazards they accepted were not a desperate alternative to, but an accepted part of, an orderly life.

By the 1770's that situation had become characteristically American. The men who moved along the northern and southern frontiers were not simply isolated drifters, placeless individuals, cut loose from any ties. They were often the sons of respectable families who left decent homes, not driven away but drawn on by impatience with the limits of the present. As a matter of course they subjected themselves to hardship and danger, strengthened as they were by the certainty of a limitless future. Habituated to a landscape without horizons, they had no fear of venturing into the unknown distances.

That situation the Nantucket whalemen shared with the Virginia planter. So the young Washington, well connected by good family, hardly hesitated to take himself off to the wilderness, abandoning comfort for the life of the shelterless forest and exchanging the company of the cultivated local gentry at Mount Vernon for that of rude trappers and Indians. It was a matter of course that such men should put in the balance the security of what they already had as against the hazards of a boundless potential.

At every level of society the speculative temperament asserted itself. The son of the prosperous merchant was more likely to go to sea than to college; he carried his wares in little craft subject to all the hazards of the elements, from port to port, appeasing hostile officials, negotiating with strangers, his mind ever occupied in calculation, his will ever hardened to gain. What fortune he accumulated was never secure, but always passed through his hands back to new enterprises. The farmer and artisan could fall in with no rhythm of production, they could not adjust to a regular round of sowing and reaping, of building and making. They too were occupied in the effort to extend themselves. They borrowed and lent, worked to save and saved to invest, driven on by the hope of great winnings, yet recognizing the possibility of great losings.

None of them liked the necessity. All their dreams revealed occasional glimpses of a distant resting place which offered surcease from their constant striving; there the husbandman divided the fruits of his fields with his family, the patriarchal master graciously guided the operations of his great plantation, the merchant neatly balanced his books and all was contentment, harmony and peace. Such wss the stability and order these people valued. But there was no confusing dreams with the reality of constant striving and ever-present danger. A situation that compelled men who cherished security constantly to seek out and to take risks formed the character of the Americans.

The willingness to accept risks had originated in the very nature of the first settlement and had been perpetuated by a society that allowed few individuals stability enough to relax in the security of exemption from further hazards. All was and remained precarious; whatever was achieved was not enough to sustain itself without further effort. Nothing stood of itself. Ceaseless striving and mobility were necessary to hold on, for only expansion could preserve what had already been created. The venture to the South Seas or to the Ohio wilderness was necessary to keep the Nantucket home or Mount Vernon from crumbling.

The risk and the constant strain of taking it were tolerable because there was a reasonable chance of reward. Space and opportunity—and therefore hope—were abundant. Every man, whatever his past, could have a future. Europeans became Americans because they no sooner arrived than they immediately felt the effects of plenty. Their toils were no less heavy than before but of a very different nature. They had put behind them involuntary idleness, servile dependence, penury and useless labor. An ample subsistence was within reach. They became landowners and for the first time in their lives, counted for something. *They ceased to be ciphers and felt themselves men because they were treated as such.* They were then Americans.

The sense of nationality was essentially the awareness of the common situation they shared. They recognized one another not by the identity of their antecedents, nor by similarities in appearance, habits, manners, or institutions, but by those traits of character that came from the effort to maintain a balance between the longing for stability and the exposure to risks. This was their environment and the environment alone molded the nature of men and established the differences among species.

Therefore it was possible for the foreign-born to come off the boat and be transformed immediately into Americans, as Paine was and as countless later immigrants would be. Indeed some could identify themselves with the nation and already be American before even leaving the Old World, if the circumstances of their own lives projected them into the same precarious situation. That identification brought scores of Europeans to fight in the revolutionary armies; and it would continue to pull others across the Atlantic on into the nineteenth century.

Independence gave political form to American nationality and deepened the characteristic traits associated with it. Pride in the achievement of having humbled the great empire, confidence in the ability to do without the trappings of traditional monarchy, and faith in man's capacity for fresh creation stimulated every imagination. It was only necessary to be daring enough! Any risk was worthwhile; and there were no limits to what the independent citizens of a republic could do.

The travelers set themselves ever more distant goals. One of Jefferson's neighbors in Virginia took to dreaming in 1792 of an overland route to the Pacific. He was only eighteen then, of a good family, bright and attractive, with every prospect before him. But he would not settle down to planting. It was ten years before Meriwether Lewis had his chance to make that long tedious journey westward to the mouth of the Columbia River. President Jefferson, who had dispatched him, no doubt remembered another genius who had also yearned to lay eyes on the Pacific. John Ledyard had sailed with Cook to the South Seas, but refused to serve the British against his countrymen. A romantic escape; wanderings through Europe; a meeting with Jefferson and John Paul Jones in Paris; then Ledyard had his idea. He would walk eastward across Russia and Siberia. He left England in 1786, passed through Norway, Sweden, and Lapland to St. Petersburg, reached Yakutsk in 1787 and Irkutsk in 1788, then, seized by order of the suspicious empress, was sent back to Poland. Frustrated, he took it into his head to locate the sources of the Niger and never returned to his native Connecticut. For such men the wish to add to knowledge was but a way of describing their restless curiosity.

Everywhere the pace of movement quickened. Settlers in the thousands hastened to the West; merchants sent their ships along hitherto untraveled lands to remote harbors; and every type of fresh enterprise attracted speculative investors. They could hardly wait, any of them, to expose themselves to risk. They were now conscious of their newness as a people; new principles animated them; and they had to assert themselves in new ideas and new achievements.

The awareness of their peculiar situation which shaped their character as a people gave a national meaning to the culture and institutions of the Americans. The looseness of their society and their desire for order, the local sources of political power and the concern with individual rights, the disregard for tradition and the eagerness for new knowledge, the tolerance of difference and the concern with ethical behavior were the accommodations of men who lived precariously in an environment that did not limit their future.

The study of the American culture and character has been a lifelong interest of GEORGE WILSON PIERSON (b. 1904), Larned Professor of History at Yale University since 1946. His study *Tocqueville and Beaumont in America* (1938) follows the journals of Tocqueville as he explored and sought to understand the nature of the American character. Pierson finds a partial answer in what he calls the "M-Factor," that is, movement, migration, and mobility, all of which he sees playing a significant and lasting role in the forging of the American.*

George Wilson Pierson

Mobile Americans

Is there any such thing as "National Character"? In particular, is there, or has there ever been, an American Character? Many critics question, or even deny the idea. Students of American civilization generally seem to start out by thinking there must be an American Character. But then they encounter great difficulties in defining this character—that is, they find too many different or contradictory types, none of the types unique, all of them appearing also in other cultures, a few of them perhaps unstable across the years. The result? Conscientious scholars are driven to despair, and decide that American society is neither consistent nor original nor completely different; therefore we have no distinctive character.

Now this, I submit, may be just a little foolish. For theoretically it isn't scientific, and practically it doesn't make sense. Theoretically, is it not a poor kind of science which says that, because you and I cannot wholly know a thing or exactly define it, it doesn't exist? Just because we cannot scientifically define Americanism would seem a quite insufficient reason for ignoring its existence. What has not existed, rather, may be that intuition of causes, that exact grasp of detail, that art of proportion, that science of social structure, which will enable us to say: this is, in a sum total way, different, *sui generis,* peculiar. After all, a combination does not have to be unique in all its elements, or even in a single one of these elements,

*From George Wilson Pierson, "The M-Factor in American History," *American Quarterly,* XIV, No. 2, Pt. 2 (Summer, 1962), pp. 275–289. Copyright 1962, Trustees of the University of Pennsylvania. Footnote omitted.

to be different in sum total. I will assert that theoretically there may be an American Character, even though that character may have been composed of familiar elements, even though it is only the proportions which have been different, even though the resulting society may be mixed, contradictory, pluralistic, unjelled. The very indeterminism of a society may be a distinguishing mark. Theoretically, I see no barrier to believing that an American Character may exist.

On the contrary, on the grounds of common sense, I see many reasons to believe that there is and has been an American Character, for one thing because the most intelligent thinkers and observers have thought so, and have kept on thinking so, across the years. These observers may have differed in the labels they attached to us, they may have argued about the causes of our American peculiarities, but every one of them has thought that the Americans are a little odd in their psychology, and a little different in their social institutions. Crèvecoeur went so far as to call the American a "New Man." And he defined this new man as the Progressive: "He is an American who leaves behind his ancient prejudices and manners." But whatever the definition, from Crèvecoeur to Tocqueville and to André Siegfried, from Dickens to Bryce to Denis Brogan, from Lieber to Keyserling or Robert Jungk, the most thoughtful commentators have asserted that there is and has been (and, alas, will continue to be) an American Character.

What caused this Americanism to emerge? Many things, no doubt; far too many even to list in this paper. So I shall confine my attention to a single prevailing characteristic of our people: the migration factor in our history, our excessive mobility. Yet before I take up the Moving American, allow me to recall some classic interpretations which have exercised a strong influence on the writing of American history, and on thinking about America generally.

How are Americans different? In the beginning was the Word, and the Word had it that we were a Chosen People, a seed sifted out of the populations of Europe, a community of saints destined to create a better society on this earth. Like the Israelites of old, we were a people under divine command. As we sang in the old hymn: "O God, beneath thy guiding hand our exiled fathers crossed the sea!"

After about one hundred and fifty years, there succeeded to this Biblical interpretation the thought that, if we were not always more holy, we were at least more free. As an independent nation, our destiny was to bring liberty, self-government, republicanism, the art of federal decentralization to the succor of oppressed mankind. So to the religious mission there succeeded a political mission—which was what Alexis de Tocqueville came to study.

From the beginning, also, there had always been an economic mission. America was El Dorado: the golden opportunity, the country of get-rich-quick, the land of the second chance, the asylum for the poverty-stricken. So as foreign and native observers alike commented, America was (1) the land of goodness, (2) the land of liberty, and (3) the land of plenty.

For a long while these three national myths satisfied. Toward the end of the nineteenth century, however, there emerged a series of more sophisticated, or "scientific," explanations, and, in particular, one which has exercised enormous influence. What was it changed Europeans into Americans?

For historians of the past generation, the Frontier Hypothesis of Frederick

Jackson Turner supplied the classic answer. It was the *frontier* experience which made us different. That is, it was our struggle with the wilderness—it was exploiting the vast free lands of the interior—it was freeing ourselves from the past, "breaking the cake of custom," leaving behind the fetters of settled society and the refinements of civilization to start over again in the woods—it was the lonely pioneers chopping out clearings on the road westward—it was getting together with other pioneers to rebuild a simpler, freer society—it was pulling up stakes and repeating the process—it was moving and moving again until in 1890 the free land and the West were all used up. On the frontier, said Turner, society became atomic, individualism flourished, democracy was generated, national legislation was encouraged. The opportunities of the West also opened a gate of escape for the oppressed of the East, and so contributed to the democratization and Americanization of the seaboard. The frontier also transformed personal character. As Turner phrased it:

> That coarseness and strength combined with acuteness and inquisitiveness; that practical, inventive turn of mind, quick to find expedients; that masterful grasp of material things, lacking in the artistic but powerful to effect great ends; that restless, nervous energy; that dominant individualism, working for good and evil, and withal that buoyancy and exuberance which comes with freedom—these are traits of the frontier, or traits called out elsewhere because of the existence of the frontier.

In effect, said Turner, it was primarily the molding influence of the Frontier which had transformed so many European materials into a new American amalgam. In his oft-quoted phrase, the frontier was "the line of most rapid and effective Americanization."

For a long while this satisfied. But about thirty years ago, when Turner died, and his imaginative idea was making its way into popular speech, and Franklin Delano Roosevelt was using the disappearance of the frontier to justify a welfare state, a number of people discovered political reasons for questioning the doctrine. Historians themselves grew uneasy. For one thing, the hypothesis seemed too nationalistic, too provincial. For another, the Frontier concept embraced too many overlapping or discordant influences. Again, the frontier cause seemed to be credited with inconsistent results: it made Americans both sectional and nationalistic, cooperative and individualistic, repetitive yet original. Once again, one wondered how many Americans could have been affected. And how were we to stay American after 1890, when the frontier disappeared? In the upshot, the frontier theory seemed to explain far too much by far too little.

Yet, for all this, it was a difficult theory to discard. For if the frontier did not produce the effects ascribed to it, what did?

I believe we now have at least a small part of the answer. It has been hinted by many perceptive observers, not least by Tocqueville or by Francis Lieber or by Sarmiento. I call it the M-Factor in American history.

What made and kept us different was not just the wildness of the North American continent, nor its vast empty spaces, nor even its wealth of resources, powerful as must have been those influences. No. It was, first of all, the M-Factor: the factor of movement, migration, mobility. Colonization was one part of it; immigration, another; the westward movement itself was a fraction, but only a fraction, of the whole. This whole began with many old-world uprootings. It gathered force with the transatlantic passage. It flooded on to the farmlands of the mid-continent. But increasingly it meant movement also *away* from the frontier, from farm to town, from region to region, from city to city. Individuals, families, churches, villages, on occasion whole countrysides have participated—and continue to participate. Francis Lieber said that in America he felt as if tied to the arms of a windmill. To him, movement had become our "historical task." And Sarmiento was so staggered by our propensity for traveling around that he predicted that, if the trump of doom were suddenly to sound, it would suprise two-thirds of the Americans, out on the roads like ants.

In all this, I repeat, the frontier played an important but limited part. For if people moved to the frontier, they moved also before there was a frontier, moved behind and away from the frontier, and kept on moving even more enthusiastically when the frontier closed.

Let us put it this way: Frederick Jackson Turner was a great poet-historian, who more than half sensed the power that was in migration, but then imprisoned this giant in the rough homespun of the vanishing pioneers. So we of a later generation must once again return to the great question: What has made and still makes Europeans into restless Americans? I venture herewith some tentative speculations, in the hope that we will find in them ideas worth working out.

My basic proposition is obvious: Movement means change. To transfer is in some part to transform. *"Wanderung meint wandlung,"* as the Germans put it. And all forms of movement, from mass exodus to simple milling around, have shared in this subtle process of alteration.

Why should motion cause change? First, because *institutions* do not move easily. A few will be destroyed; many more are damaged; nearly all are shaken, and have to be pruned, simplified, or otherwise adjusted to survive the transplanting. To a degree *displacement* means *replacement* of institutions.

Why again should migration cause modification? Because the migrants are not average people. As a group they do not represent a fair cross-section of the society they are leaving; as individuals they tend toward exaggerations of one sort or another; as settlers they won't wish to reproduce the society they have left, or succeed in reproducing it even should they so desire.

This brings us to the third great reason for change, the new circumstances: that is, the hardships and accidents of the crossing, the strangers encountered on the road, the unaccustomed climate and geography of their new environment. Movement means exposure, and successive exposures compel unexpected changes.

It may be urged that more credit should go to the strangers and the new countries. Or it may be observed that migrations are often the result or the symptom of changes that have already taken place in the parent society. And with both these ideas I agree. On the one hand, many immigrants were Americanized only long after they got over. On the other, not a few American types, like the puritan and the businessman, had already appeared in sixteenth-century Europe. So migration served both as prologue and as epilogue; it has been the means of change and the effect of change (as well as the cause). Yet no movement of people or institutions, however started or motivated, can take place without further alterations. For migration selects special types for moving; it subjects them to exceptional strains on the journey; and it then compels them to rebuild, with liberty to choose or refuse from the mail-order catalogue of Western experience. On top of all that, repeated movements, such as we in our country have known, seem to have a cumulative, or progressive, effect.

What parts of a civilization, what elements in a society, does the M-Factor attack? Apparently, all parts. Before his death Ellsworth Huntington, who was one of the earliest American scientists to become curious about this phenomenon, came to see in migration a selective force so strong that it affected the stock and temperament of a people as well as its culture. After some hesitations, I believe we will concur. For I believe it can be demonstrated that movement changes the physical population, the institutions and group structures, the social habits and traditions, the personal character and attitudes of the migrants.

Allow me to offer some random, familiar illustrations at this point.

The American population? It was formed and re-formed by migration. To begin with we were all immigrants. Moreover, because the Atlantic was open, people from many lands and nations came to these shores, until we were the leading conglomerate of the West, a Rainbow Division of Europe. Political scientists call us a pluralistic society. Sociologists find culture conflicts endemic.

Again because the migrants did not all come at once, but in intermittent surges, and because in free movements the later comers, as strangers, are handicapped and must enter the lower levels of their class and occupation, the natives or earlier-comers have repeatedly found themselves pushed upstairs, to the more skilled jobs, to the managerial posts, to the position of employers and capitalists. At the same time, moving upstairs was difficult, so difficult that the older stock felt it had to cut down on the number of its own children, if it was to graduate them into the higher levels of living—so difficult that the next-to-last comers tended to resent the labor competition of the newcomers and tried to exclude them. Thus the Yankees industrialized with the aid of other people's children. Meanwhile these laboring generations, as they matured, tried to keep the jobs for themselves and, whether as skilled artisans or later trade union bosses, as Know-Nothings in the 1850s or McCarthyites a century later, became the strongest champions of immigration restriction, the most suspicious of new foreigners, the uncompromising 100 percenters. So from 1820 to 1920 what ought to have been for the Anglo-American population a series of European additions became instead a progressive physical substitution. And after 1920 the freedom to immigrate was shut off by the votes of the very groups which had benefited from it earlier. But why did not and has not this stepladder movement of infiltration produced a stratified, hierarchical, skyscraper society? The answer is again the M-Factor, but this time internal migration. Inside, the freedom to move remained, and a man could get out of his cellar in town by building a one-story cabin up-country, or he could come off his eroded acres into Chicago, where the rising buildings and professions had elevators in them.

If we now turn from questions of nationality and occupation to the age and sex characteristics of our population, we find that here, too, the M-Factor has left deep marks. For three hundred years, or at least until the great depression, we were a young country. We boasted of it. Foreigners rarely failed to mention the childlike innocence, the boyish enthusiasm, the youthful drive and bustle and activity-for-activity's sake of these strange Americans. The youth of America, quipped Oscar Wilde, is its oldest tradition. And perhaps we were guilty of a certain "shortage of adults." At least the demographers have proved that our Constitution was made for adolescents—as late as 1820 the median age of the population was only 16 years, and it was not until well into the twentieth century that that median soared above 25. That is, it was only after preventive medicine had started to prolong the lives of the infirm, and immigration restriction had cut down on the annual influx of bachelors and young marrieds, that we first really began to feel middle-aged. How does the M-Factor figure in this? Well, students of migration have rediscovered the fact that it is overwhelmingly the young, between the ages of 15 and 25, who move—and in the first waves or pioneer phases, it is primarily the young men. The frontiers, whether of farm or factory, start emphatically male (*Oh Susannah, don't you cry for me!*).

Yet the men were not to have it all their own way, for the M-Factor can give things a sardonic twist. Migration has perennially represented rebellion against past tyrannies or authorities, against the father no less than against the lord or priest, against the husband no less than against the father. Thus, after the first settlements had been established, the open spaces and open opportunities of this country just invited the younger generation to leave home and strike out on their own, and the able young men accepted the invitation. Even today it is the rare son of ability who does not insist on leaving the town where he was born to try to make his way in a larger world. Meanwhile the pioneer women, being scarce as well as weak, found that they had inadvertently acquired a scarcity value. For them, as well as for the children, migration meant progressive emancipation—an emancipation eventually crowned by woman suffrage, Mother's Day and much symbolic statuary. Thus, as our lonely forefathers pushed relentlessly westward, and the idea of equality came galloping up behind, the Pioneer Mother replaced the Pilgrim Father on the sculptor's pedestal in the town square. (Whether the statuesque Miss America has now replaced her bronzed mother in the popular imagination I leave to braver men to say—we may note only the querulous complaints of our English and Continental friends that we are today a woman-run and child-dominated subcivilization.)

If we next pursue the M-Factor from our population to our economy, what will we find? An economy in which transportation has loomed extraordinarily large—witness the railroads, the automobile age and the airplane industry of today—witness also in our myths how prairie schooners and pony express, paddle wheelers and the long whistle of the trains, Ford cars and the Spirit of St. Louis have entered into the folklore of our people.

The wheels are singing on the railroad track
If you go, you can't come back.
Hear the whistle blow.

For Americans, it has been said, the automobile restates a national principle, since, after all, the settler was the first auto-mobile. In the U.S. a mile is something to put behind you. Where else would you find a place named Stillwater Junction?

More soberly, if our interest runs rather to our religious peculiarities, it might be observed that the need for settlers, and the ease of exit and entrance from one colony to the other, made toleration and disestablishment of churches almost inevitable from the start. The same ease of escape then long made it difficult for the states to impose adequate taxation, or any other really burdensome regulation, on their footloose citizens. A Virginian did not have to stay in Virginia. A Yorker could go to Michigan. If a business failed, or a marriage, the simplest thing was to decamp. Other states would welcome you. So . . . Reno became a monument to our vagrant fancies in matters matrimonial.

Again, politically our moving habits not only made possible but reinforced a decentralizing, federal tendency. Legally, the absence of customary law in the new settlements must have fostered the excessive American dependence on statute law. Migration also splintered our first establishments of higher education, in the sense that it led to the founding of many colleges instead of concentration on a few national universities. Thus my own institution, through the efforts of its migrating graduates, became a mother of colleges a full century before it could accumulate enough substance in New Haven to rival the great foundations of Europe. Finally, our peculiar instability of family homesite, and the lack of a national capital or home, shifted emotional loyalties to things that could be carried with us, such as declarations of principle and constitutional theories. And eventually, to bind ourselves together, we were forced to insist with an unusual, almost tyrannical, emphasis on such assimilative codes and social practices as are commonly summed up in that telltale phrase: "The American WAY of Life."

But enough of such random illustrations.

Let us now proceed to ask, on a more systematic basis, how, just how, have migration and movement acted to convert Europeans into something rich and strange?

Considering the matter first on a broad social scale, I would propose that the M-Factor has been (turn by turn or even all at once): (1) the great Eliminator; (2) the persistent Distorter; (3) an arch-Conservator; (4) an almost irresistible Disintegrator or Atomizer; (5) a heart Stimulant or Energizer; and (6) the prime source of Optimism in the American atmosphere, a never-failing ozone of hope. Also, (7) the Secularizer and Externalizer of our beliefs, and (8) the Equalizer and Democratizer of social classes. Indeed a little reflection will suggest still other ways in which migration has shaken its European ingredients into new patterns. But on this occasion let us consider merely some of these eight, with just a hint or two of historic events by way of illumination.

Migration was the great Eliminator? Nothing could be plainer. In theory you can't take everything with you when you move. Some goods are too bulky or delicate to be put on ship; some household possessions will fall out of the covered wagon. Again, in a free migration, not all elements in a society will wish to move; the dregs will be too spiritless and impoverished to emigrate unaided; the ruling classes entirely too successful and satisfied. Check this theory against history and what do we find? In the early colonization there came out of England the rising middle classes, with some admixture of the lowest elements, but with only a few aristocratic leaders. Ours started, therefore, as a decapitated society, virtually without nobles or bishops, judges or learned lawyers, artists, playwrights or great poets. Taking a hopeful view, a student of mine once maintained that settlement transferred the accent from *nobility* to *ability*. Considering the transfer culturally, however, one must recognize a tragic impoverishment. Despite all our gains of goodness or plenty or freedom, the men of the highest attainments and greatest skills had stayed home—and with them their arts and refinements, their leisure-class culture. The same process of abandonment, of flight from the elite and their standards, would be discernible later in the settlement of the West. Axiomatically, the fine arts, the theoretical sciences, the most advanced tools and machinery, are not found or produced on moving frontiers. Like war or fire or inflation, migration has been a great destroyer of inherited treasure.

At first glance such destruction may seem only temporary, to be replaced "when we have time." Yet meanwhile some elements are missing, the balance is changed, the old society has been distorted—and before long one may get reconciled to doing without. On top of this, the M-Factor has promoted distortion in an even more drastic way. For moving forces the reclassification of values. Why? Because the land of destination attracts more strongly for one or two presumed goods than for the others (as for economic opportunity perhaps, or political freedom, or the right to worship in one's own way). So if a family is to go, they have to believe, or persuade themselves, that the particular goods to be realized are more important to them than all the other social goods, which may be diminished, or even be left behind altogether. If similar movements are made by later generations for like reasons, then these cherished values may rise almost to the status of holy commandments or natural rights, and in the nineteenth century become the polar magnets in a new value system. By elimination and wilful distortion a moving people becomes a narrower society: thinner and shallower, yet in some things much more intense.

This calls attention to a third and almost paradoxical characteristic of migration: its conservatism. People moved to save as well as to improve. But when they found they couldn't take everything with them, then a curious thing often happened. They came to value even more highly what they had succeeded in preserving. Having suffered such privations, having sacrificed so many other possessions, they clung to what was saved with a fiercer passion. Witness the Puritans with their Wilderness Zion, the Mormons under Brigham Young, or even Turner's leapfrogging pioneers. For these last, as for so many others, it had become easier to move than to change their vocation, their habits, their antiquated methods. To put this bluntly, for them the cheap lands of the West made it easier to keep on with their soil-mining and strip-farming, and possible to avoid such painful changes as learning a proper care of the land, or the new crop rotation of the advanced parts of Europe and the East. So for the American farmer—or agriculturally speaking—the westward movement became the great postponement of American history. They profited personally, but it was a postponement nonetheless—just as in the flight of the New England textile industry to the South in our times. In France, before De Gaulle, the peasant and small shopkeeper clung stubbornly to his land or shop, but politically moved constantly to the left. That is, economically, he might be a selfish reactionary, and even vote for Poujade, but by changing the name of his party leftward he was sure he was making "progress." Did not some of our American pioneers give themselves the same feeling of progress by moving westward? Migration, I would suggest, could be a way of promoting change—and of avoiding it, too. Flight can be an escape from the future as well as from the past.

The M-Factor, we must next realize, was an almost irresistible Disintegrator or Atomizer. Few authoritarian institutions from Europe could stand the strain of Atlantic distances or the explosion of

American space. So either they decentralized or died. Witness the early church. In Virginia the episcopal organization proved so little suited to the far-flung tobacco plantations that the Church of England almost withered away, whereas in New England the Puritan branch of the same church developed a localized or Congregational organization, and flourished. Then, later, when the Irish immigration poured life and vigor into American Catholicism, the hierarchy, intuitively recognizing that moving out on the lands might cripple the Church as well as weaken the individual's faith, did their best to hold the new arrivals in the seaport towns, at least until some interior communities could be effectively churched. Ultimately, I believe it will be found that our Catholics have moved less often, less widely and less soon than their Protestant neighbors, hence have missed certain corrosive acids and opportunities in the M-Factor.

One of these opportunities, of course, was to stand on your own feet, to make your own way, and if need be to move again. In our expanding settlements the arm of the State (like the authority of the bishops) shriveled, and a kind of physical individualism sprouted. On the trail, society tended to break down into chance parties of moving families or individuals. And at the destination everything was to be reconstructed. It took energy and courage to move, and more energy to make the move succeed. Hence migration was a great stimulant to action—and when such action repeatedly succeeded (or, as we may say, "worked"), then perhaps the beginnings of a habit of action had been established, both for oneself and for one's neighbor. The American reputation for activism, as for self-help and neighborly helpfulness, surely needs no underlining.

Migration was not only the Destroyer, Distorter, Conservator, Atomizer and Energizer of western society, but its most effective "Optimizer." First of all, out of the welter of old-world classes and temperaments it selected the up-and-coming and the hopeful. Pessimists didn't bother; you had to be an optimist to move. Next it required sacrifice and waiting, and so captured many believers, the men of faith. Finally, it rewarded the successful—and those who weren't lucky were given a second try. America the Golden was the land of the second chance. And from failure it offered a full timetable of escapes.

I realize that is it customary at this point to do a ritualistic dance around the statue of the golden calf—and credit our optimism or success primarily to the sheer wealth of the continent. But if we did become a "people of plenty," and if that plenty left its mark even on the size of our automobiles, let us not forget that the beginnings were almost invariably hard, and what the land long offered most of was tough places and violent weather. What kind of plenty was it converted the gravel patch of New England into smiling farms? Lots of hard work, I should say, and plenty of faith. Again, who but a lunkheaded optimist would grow wheat in Kansas? Or who in his right mind would go settle in Dakota? No. The Black Hills gold and the U.S. farm bounties, these bonanzas were later and almost accidental discoveries. In my book, optimism made more states than vice versa. Many a town existed first, or only, in the imagination. "Boost, don't knock" has been the slogan of new communities just abuilding, and the booster is Mr. Johnny-come-lately. We began as migrants, that is, wishful thinkers, and each wave of immigration, each boatload from abroad, brought us fresh injections of this heart stimulant. For Europe's poor, the freedom to come changed "tomorrow" from a threat into a promise. For its men of faith, the act of moving and moving again substituted "the future" for "the heavenly hereafter." And with time the mission of American idealists came to be in and for this world. From infant damnation to the social gospel is but a long tramp.

I hope I may be forgiven if I now pass over the secularizing and externalizing influences of mobility (which Sorokin has explored) in favor of its equalitarian and leveling effects. For these democratic tendencies seem to me particularly important, and I have stumbled on some odd illustrations.

Here the theoretical argument would be that the M-Factors are often democratic in their consequences, first because for the lower classes emigration means *"getting out from under,"* the first step on the road up; secondly because the hardships of the journey are no respecters of birth (witness the miserable failure of the early "Gentlemen" of the Jamestown Colony in Virginia). In the third place, and most significantly, the process of resettlement is a process of making new mixtures, out of a gathering of strangers, each without authority, credentials, reputation or other priority than that of arrival. In a new community (frontier or town) family and past performance hardly count. Everyone has to make his own mark, and stands equal with his fellow-strangers. The social competition, as it were, starts over, with all the camaraderie and "gamesmanship" of a new catch-as-catch-can. Migration has been a great Mixmaster. And mixtures of anonymous elements are necessarily more democratic, at least at first. So much for doctrine. Now for my illustrations.

My first illustration, if you will allow the personal reference, comes out of an effort to understand my own university. How explain Yale College of the 1890s, a college that prided itself on its democracy? It is true there were a few Whitneys, Vanderbilts or Harknesses, with social pretentions and inordinate allowances. Yet evidently the game was wide open, and any self-help student from no matter how humble a background or obscure a school had a chance to show what he could do and rise to the top and be the honor man in the Senior Society elections, if he had what it took. Now how was it possible that a college like Yale, with almost two hundred years of tradition and family attachments, could still offer so fair and square an opportunity to all comers? Because Yale was, in a sense, an annually renewed community, and because its constituents came, not just from arond New Haven or New England but from all over the country, without prior knowledge of each other or claims to authority. It was a skeptical Harvard professor, European born, who first taught me this truth. Listen to George Santayana:

> The relations of one Yale student to another are completely simple and direct. They are like passengers in a ship. . . . They live in a sort of primitive brotherhood with a ready enthusiasm for every good or bad project, and a contagious good humor.
>
> . . . Nothing could be more American. . . . Here is sound, healthy principle, but no scrupulousness, love of life, trust in success, a ready jocoseness, a democratic amiability, and a radiant conviction that there is nothing better than oneself. It is a boyish type of character, earnest and quick in things practical, hasty and frivolous in things intellectual, but the boyishness is a healthy one, and in a young man, as in a young nation, it is perfection to have only the faults of youth.

What Yale College and the Frontier, and indeed much of the rest of America, had in common, Santayana suggests, was young Americans in a new mixture.

If this first illustration comes with a strange sound, let me hasten to propose my second. It concerns dogs. In France, on sabbatical a few years ago, I seemed to run into only two kinds of dogs. One was the pampered, pedigreed poodle, sitting with his mistress in the restaurants, even eating from her plate: the fine flower of canine aristocracy, and most grandly indifferent to strangers. The second type was nondescript and fierce, the savage watchdog at peasant doorway or château gate, guarding the family domain and inherited possessions, *"les situations acquises."* This character disliked strangers on sight, and promptly tried to chew them up. After one or two close calls with such receptionists, I came back to the States—and found dogs of all sorts of ancestry, chiefly mixed. But what they showed mostly was curiosity, and a sort of friendly expectancy. Their tails said: "Howdy, stranger." For they were not guarding any particular place. They belonged to traveling men, and had been around.

My third illumination, if we can call it that, concerns money. Foreigners still accuse us of being excessively money-minded, of measuring everything by the almighty dollar. Our defenders answer: it's not the money, it's the power and the achievement. You make a million to prove you're a man; then, like as not, you give it away. After all, you can't take it with you.

Yet can't you? As I was once thinking about the M-Factor, it suddenly came to me that on a journey, or in a new community, money was one of the few things that you could take along. Cash took the place of your pedigree or family letter of credit. It spoke with a certain authority, East or West. Money was power? Yes. But especially it was currency: the power that you could take with you. So on the moving frontier, in the new towns, it was differentiation by dollars that first disturbed the democracy of new mixtures.

Having got diverted by some of the social consequences of the M-Factor, I cannot do justice to some of the most interesting effects of all: the influence of migration on personal character and attitudes. In the moment remaining let me merely suggest possibilities.

Was it not the psychological imperatives of migration, even more than frontier land, that helped make and keep us a nation of optimists? Was it not the physical demands of colonization and resettlement, as well as Calvinism and middle-class origins, that made us into such a nation of workers, activists, materialists, instrumentalists? The difference between what André Siegfried calls "homo faber" or the American, and homo sapiens or the European, is it not perhaps that one of these characters has been sitting still? Whereas we, poor pilgrims, have itching feet. Restless to start with, we have become more so with repeated displacement. *Here today and gone tomorrow.* The wandering mania has got into our blood, our houses, our attention, our very ways of speech. *Come on! Get going! Don't be a stick-in-the-mud! You don't want to get left, do you? It's a good year to make the move. So long! I don't know where I'm going, but I'm on my way. Anywhere I hang my hat is home, sweet home, to me.*

In the revealing American vernacular it is impressive to observe how many things are defined in terms of movement. A man *on the road* to success is a *comer,* a *go-getter. That's going some,* we say—and by and by we listen for the magic words that we also have *arrived.* So also with failure. *He missed the bus.* Or, *he missed the boat. He is not getting anywhere. She got left in the lurch. He got bogged down with administration.* A man who is growing old is *slowing up,* and then by and by he reaches *the end of the trail.* Death itself used to be spoken of as *crossing the divide.*

Reinforcing the testimony of our vernacular are our social habits. Unable to stay put, thrown among fellow transients, having newcomers flood in about us, we have perforce become hospitable, and genial with strangers. Not knowing their ancestry, and caring less, first names have been all we needed. There is a fellowship in our country, known to some of you perhaps, where last names are absolutely prohibited. And, incidentally, this illustrates another American trait: our propensity for "joining." Lonely from disassociation, we will make ten lodges grow where but one *bierstube* stood before. Frightened and not quite able to bear our independence, we oscillate between assertiveness and timidity, between an almost violent aggression and an almost cowardly conformity. Imaginative and suggestible, we are notorious for our fads and our instability. Insecure in our values, we have become adept at inventing dogmas to comfort ourselves. Not quite sure that our abandonment of the old world and of the past was justified, we have long been haunted by ambivalent feelings: a mixture of scorn and guilt complex about the older civilizations of Europe.

"It is a complex fate, being an American," said Henry James, "and one of the responsibilities it entails is fighting against a superstitious valuation of Europe." Ralph Waldo Emerson felt the same way: "Can we never extract the tapeworm of Europe from the brain of our countrymen?"

Finally, because migration appealed for diverse reasons especially to extremists—to saints and real sinners, to fundamentalists and free thinkers, to dreamers and "tough bastards," to groupists and individualists side by side—our society has never received its fair share of balanced, equable, middle-of-the-road temperaments, but has been shot through with violent contradictions. Hence so many of our seeming inconsistencies, to this very day.

To me the migrant seems not a single or a simple character, but is he not recognizably different—and American?

Paradoxically, if we turn up the other side of the coin, there are the Europeans, fearful of becoming Americanized. Is this entirely out of weakness, or envy, or admiration? Hardly. Let us rather take note of a curious and unappreciated development. In the last generation mobility has swept the continent. With their *vacances payês,* their *campings,* their folkwagons, our cousins have found a new freedom. So, if today there is Americanization in Europe, and if our ways of life seem to be coming closer together, may it not be in part because the Old World societies are as never before in movement, and because Siegfried's "homo sapiens," too, is taking to the roads?

Suggested Readings

A great many volumes written about the United States touch obliquely, if not directly, upon the character of the American people. This list of suggestions for further reading does not attempt, therefore, to be inclusive, but offers a limited number of specific readings which will broaden the reader's background in each of the several areas covered in this volume.

An excellent introduction to the English cultural heritage is found in Wallace Notestein, *The English People On the Eve of Colonization: 1603–1630* (New York, 1954), particularly Chapters II and III, "The English Character." Notestein studies the various customs and institutional forms growing out of English character and the attitudes which were selectively transmitted to New England and Virginia. Detailed exploration of the transplantation of the European cultural heritage is found in Daniel J. Boorstin, *The Americans: The Colonial Experience* (New York, 1958). A second volume, *The Americans: The National Experience* (New York, 1965) explores the unfolding of this heritage within the natural boundaries and influences of the American continent. Howard Mumford Jones demonstrates the transfer of the European cultural heritage through the Renaissance ideals which influenced American thought and institutions in *O Strange New World—American Culture: The Formative Years* (New York, 1964). Still of value is Henry Bamford Parkes, *The American Experience* (New York, 1947), which examines the basic historical forces that influenced the American character. Of more limited use but interesting as an early collection is Dixon Ryan Fox, editor, *Sources of Culture in the Middle West: Backgrounds versus Frontier* (New York, 1934; 1964).

Some of the most fascinating commentaries on the American character appear in travel accounts written by English and European visitors to America. In addition to the fertile pages of Alexis de Tocqueville, *Democracy in America* (1835, 1840), a selection from which appears in this volume, useful information will be found in Hector St. John de Crèvecoeur, *Letters From An American Farmer* (First printed, London, 1782); Harriet Martineau, *Society in America,* 3 volumes (London, 1837); James Bryce, *The American Commonwealth,* 2 volumes) (New York, 1888); André Siegfried, *America Comes of Age* (New York, 1927) and *America at Mid-Century* (New York, 1955); and D. W. Brogan, *The American Character* (New York, 1944). Despite varying emphases, the unifying element found in all these commentaries is an underlying belief in a distinctive American character.

The Atlantic Migration: 1607-1860 (Cambridge, Mass., 1940) by Marcus Lee Hansen provides a rapid route to a better understanding of the circumstances existing in the various nations and districts from which the emigrants to America took their departure. The reception and assimilation of these migrants in America is one key to the study of character-forming influences. A more poetic presentation suggesting some of the psychological effects of migration is *The Uprooted* (Boston, 1957) by Oscar Handlin.

Those who wish to read more extensively in Frederick Jackson Turner's writings will find his essays in three collections: *The Frontier in American History* (New York, 1920; 1962), *The Significance of Sections in American History* (New York, 1932), and *The Early Writings of Frederick Jackson Turner* (Madison, 1938). An important and newly published

Turner lecture, "Some Sociological Aspects of American History," edited by Wilbur R. Jacobs in *Frederick Jackson Turner's Legacy* (San Marino, Calif., 1965) focuses directly on the social and institutional modifications wrought by the American environment. *The Rise of the New West, 1819-1829* (New York, 1906) by Turner should also prove useful. Lee Benson explores the intellectual origins of Turner's thought in *Turner and Beard: American Historical Writing Reconsidered* (Glencoe, Ill., 1960).

In *The Great Plains* (New York, 1931) Walter Prescott Webb details the influence of that geographical expanse upon American institutions and life and considers its immediate effects upon the Anglo-American. Webb broadens the application of Turner's frontier hypothesis in *The Great Frontier* (Boston, 1952).

The Turner thesis has provided stimulation for a large body of supporting and dissenting scholarship. Among those dissenting publications bearing on the question of American Character formation are Benjamin F. Wright, Jr., "American Democracy and the Frontier," *The Yale Review,* XX (December 1930), pp. 349–365, which argues that democratic characteristics of Americans are part of their European cultural heritage, and Henry Nash Smith's important study, *Virgin Land: The American West as Symbol and Myth* (Cambridge, Mass., 1950), which argues that Turner's frontier was a romanticized, mythical product of a no longer adequate agrarian intellectual tradition. The most thorough and comprehensive recent defense of Turner's work is by Ray A. Billington. His *America's Frontier Heritage* (New York, 1966), including the selection in this volume, provides a brilliant synthesis of the Turnerian controversy and reaffirms persuasively the viability of the environmental argument for a distinctive American character. Also of interest is his edited volume, *The Frontier Thesis: Valid Interpretation of American History?* New York, 1966), and *The American Frontier* (2d ed.; Washington D.C. 1965).

The serious student will want to read extensively in the area of personality and culture in order to acquire an adequate theoretical background for dealing with the whole concept of national character. Margaret Mead's review of national character studies entitled "National Character" in Sol Tax, editor, *Anthropology Today: Selections* (Chicago, 1962), pp. 396–421, and A. Irving Hallowell, "Culture, Personality, and Society" in the same volume, pp. 351–374, provide a good beginning. *The Psychological Frontiers of Society* (New York, 1945) by Abram Kardiner, and *The Cultural Background of Personality* (New York, 1945) by Ralph Linton are more extended studies which should prove useful. Another point of view is expressed by Anthony Wallace in *Culture and Personality* (New York, 1961).

Related more specifically to the American scene are these key articles: Otto Klineberg, "American Culture and American Personality: Some Methodological Considerations," *Journal of Social Issues,* VI, No. 4 (1951), pp. 40–44; Richard E. Sykes, "American Studies and the Concept of Culture: A Theory and Method," *American Quarterly,* XV, No. 2, Part 2 (Summer 1963, supplement), pp. 253–270; and Max Lerner, "The Idea of American Civilization," *Journal of Social Issues,* VII, No. 4 (1951), pp. 30–39. In addition to the selection from David Potter, *People of Plenty* (Chicago, 1954) which is reprinted in this collection, "The Study of National Character" from that volume is an important synthesis and application of many of the principles presented in these personality and culture studies. Walter P. Metzger reassesses the concept of national character and its uses in "Generalizations about National Character: An Analytical Essay" in *Generalization in the Writing of History,* Louis Gottschalk, editor (Chicago, 1963), pp. 77–102. A historiography of national character studies is presented in Thomas L. Hartshorne, *The Distorted Image: Changing Conceptions of the National Character Since Turner* (Cleveland, 1968).

Other useful and frequently cited works on American character are: George Santayana, *Character and Opinion in the United States* (New York, 1920); several studies by David Riesman, including "The Study of National Character: Some Observations on the American Case" in *Abundance for What?* (New York, 1964), *The Lonely* Crowd (New York, 1953), *Faces in the Crowd* (New Haven, 1951), and *Individualism Reconsidered* (Glencoe, Ill., 1954); Margaret Mead, *And Keep Your Powder Dry* (New York, 1942); Lee Coleman, "What is American: A Study of Alleged American Traits," *Social Forces,* XIX (May 1941), pp. 492-499; John Hague, editor, *American Character and Culture: Some Twentieth Century Perspectives* (1964); and Elting E. Morison, *The American Style: Essays in Value and Performance* (New York, 1958).

The reader seeking additional bibliographical resources touching on all aspects of the study of American character will find indispensable Michael McGiffert's *The Character of Americans* (Homewood, Ill., 1964; revised edition, 1970), which includes a comprehensive annotated list of articles and books published since 1940. This bibliography is also available in part as "Selected Writings on American National Character," *American Quarterly,* XV (Summer 1963), pp. 271–288. McGiffert has updated the bibliography to 1969 in *American Quarterly,* XXI (Summer 1969), pp. 330–349.